ENDORSEMENTS

A force of humanity, Jim has repeatedly set far-reaching examples of strength and perseverance in the human experience by impacting moments, minutes, and lifetimes next door and across the globe. Compassionate towards this selfless global agenda, Jim demonstrates an unwavering commitment to the distribution of knowledge, time, and integrity through powerfully calm words and perpetual action. Throughout the many hands and hearts touched, Jim leads to uplift, empower, and embrace life's challenges with a passion that needs no translation. Time spent with Jim is one of those experiences that leaves us with a grassroots reminder of what being human is.

DR. PARRY, Assistant to the CEO for the International Internet Alliance

(Ms. Parry worked closely with Dr. Garrow for three years. Her mother was Dr. Garrow's vice president of human resources.)

Jim Garrow is one of the most interesting people I know. Everyone has a story to tell; Jim has an epic. He has taken upon himself the burden of rescuing tens of thousands—and potentially hundreds of thousands—of girl babies who are at risk of gendercide in China. Despite the danger to himself, and the enormous financial cost, he is standing up to one of the great evils of the modern age, and bringing life and hope to people across China and around the world, through the Pink Pagoda project.

This is a story known only to a few people. Yet after I met Jim, I discovered that he, personally, is known far and wide. The old slogan about six degrees of separation is more like one or two with Jim. In other words, I started discovering that many people I knew already knew Jim, even if they didn't know about Pink Pagoda. He has a natural gift for networking, forming connections, bringing people together, and making things happen, and he puts these gifts to work generously in the service of others. It is no wonder he was such a successful entrepreneur. And when the call came to put these gifts to work saving lives, he could very easily have turned a blind eye and walked away. But he didn't, and what happened next is one of the most fascinating and exciting stories of the twenty-first century.

It is hard for us in the free West to fully understand the tragedy of China's one-child policy. It has caused grievous suffering for millions of men and women who are forced to make the most appalling choices. I long for the day the Communist Party rejects the twisted, inhumane ideology that led to its imposition and sets the Chinese people free to determine their own family sizes. In the meantime, I hope and pray that Jim Garrow and Pink Pagoda will carry on with their subversive rescue operations.

ROSS MCKITRICK, Professor of Economics, University of Guelph, Canada, RossMcKitrick.weebly.com

(Dr. Ross McKitrick is a world-renowned economist who showed by detailed analysis of the data that the claims of the "man-made global warming" acolytes were a fraudulent use of the data and showed quite the opposite of the claims. Al Gore and the leading advocates/beneficiaries of the claims will not debate Ross in public. He tears them and their claims apart.)

I am glad that Jim Garrow is one of my friends. I was his pastor, but more importantly we have been friends who have mutually encouraged and challenged each other to take steps of faith that have been courageous rather than giving in to the fears of people or circumstances. Jim has always taken faithful risks; been an outspoken advocate for the unborn, the broken, and people in need; and has taken action to bless others through his efforts, expertise, experience, and generosity. I have seen him persevere through problems and obstacles, all the while keeping a contagious realistic optimism that something can be done and accomplished even though opposition persists. In his career, he has worked and ministered in hard places, and given leadership in messy situations while bringing a breath of fresh air and challenge to see situations turn around. He has been controversial to some, at the forefront of new ideas, and willing to do things that 99 percent of the world will not attempt, and because of that he has had influence, new opportunities, and possibilities that others have not experienced. In my world, we say that was a "God thing" that just happened. Jim and I have talked about this because the smallest yes to the need of another person can create tremendous ripples that can impact countless people. This book demonstrates that life principle.

ROBIN W. PIFER, Pastor, Cedarview Alliance Church, Nepean, Ontario

(Reverend Pifer is formerly the minister of networks for the Fellowship of Evangelical Baptist Churches of Canada. He is a coach and mentor to pastors across Canada.)

I responded to meeting Jim Garrow with suspicion. He had come into a challenging situation and was too relaxed and confident. His somewhat casual appearance enhanced this impression. How could this guy be for real?

As I got to know him, I repeatedly observed that his confidence was built on two things—his uncanny ability to quickly assess the situation and the people with whom he was dealing, and his determination to do what was right. He would then move forward in doing what was right, with little patience for those who chose to play political or power games. He had strong loyalty for all those who responded to him with honesty, whether he agreed with their position or not.

Jim has paid for his "get things done right without regard for political correctness" modus operandi by being misunderstood, by being envied, by being subject to personal attack, and in some cases, by moving on because the job wasn't going to get completed in the environment that existed, and he had more to accomplish elsewhere.

Jim is constantly promoting but is more of an enthusiastic idea man than a promoter, is continually called upon to lead but is more of a creator of leaders than a leader, is a holder of strong political views but is more of a philosopher than a politician, is involved in humanitarian endeavors but is more of a vision developer than a social worker, is trained in psychology but is more of a coach than a counselor, and moves so quickly that many who encounter him do not get to know him, but to those who have the privilege of getting to know him, he is a real friend.

When I was initially trying to understand this unique guy, I sought the opinion of a trusted mutual acquaintance. He described Jim as "a rogue with integrity." If one accepts the fun-loving, mischievous definition of rogue, that is Jim. He is someone who acts differently than most in order to accomplish more than most, for the good of many. He takes his radical faith seriously and is determined to see that what is right has its rightful place in our world.

WALTER BAKER

(Walter Baker has been a teacher, a principal, and executive director of Fairhavens Bible Conference.)

This is a book about a complex man, engaged in a compromised and dangerous moral odyssey, in an ideologically incomprehensible country. Readers will be deeply moved and gladdened by Jim Garrow's unrelenting personal dedication to saving the lives of so many otherwise doomed baby girls in China. When I closed the book, and because all the Western nations have during the past half century normalized pediatric euthanasia (otherwise known as abortion), I found myself hoping Jim's story will call forth from their midst similarly dedicated citizens to take up the cause of saving innocent life.

WILLIAM D. GAIRDNER

(William D. Gairdner, PhD, is a former Olympic athlete and English professor, and the best-selling author of seven books. His books The Trouble with Canada, The War against the Family, *and* The Trouble with Democracy *are all available from BPS Books.)*

In a world where a "crisis of conscience" sometimes leads to compromise and a devaluing of convictions that some hold true, Jim Garrow stands apart. His conviction "to do no harm" has led him to save baby girls from gendercide in the People's Republic of China. "All it takes for evil to prevail is for good men to stand by and do nothing," rings so true in this world today. Prime Minister Churchill knew too well what it takes to stand for good and against evil. Dr. Garrow understood only too well that his promise before God was not a light one to take, his oath to follow God's path a serious venture into the unknown. But he was willing, able, and ready to follow the leading of his God. The rest is history and should be celebrated as outstanding on this world's stage. My wholehearted support of *The Pink Pagoda* and its record of this man's uncompromising commitment to life is given with pleasure and pride.

DR. A.B., Medical Ethics Committee, UNESCO– World Health Organization

Often times we relegate the work of God to those who call themselves "Pastors." However, God's call on our lives is for everyone who calls themselves a follower of Jesus Christ. *The Pink Pagoda* is about a layman educator who listened to the heart of God and responded to the need to save a baby from infanticide. Jim Garrow decided to be obedient to God and over 40,000 baby girls live today as a result. By trusting God and following His leading, we can change this world.

DR. JIM GARLOW

Dr. and Mrs. Garlow are the parents of four adopted children. Jim is Senior Pastor at Skyline Church and Chairman at Renewing American Leadership.

The Pink Pagoda tells the tale of a modern-day hero saving baby girls from gendercide in the People's Republic of China. In 2009, Jim Garrow was nominated for the Nobel Peace Prize by a grateful grandfather who wanted the world to know about this giant on the world's stage, standing up at great personal cost to China's war against its daughters. Instead the world gasped at the prize going to a fraud like Barack Obama, who had done nothing other than winning an election with great promises and no deeds. The travesty here is that real heroism was bypassed and the real meaning of the Nobel Peace Prize was trashed in the eyes of the world. Perhaps the Nobel organization will take a second look at the work of Dr. Garrow and fix this error in a subsequent year. Real heroes deserve to win in the end.

JEROME CORSI, best-selling author of *Where's the Birth Certificate?*

(Where's the Birth Certificate? *is the seminal work of research that exposed the fraud of Barack Hussein Obama.)*

THE PINK PAGODA

THE
PINK
PAGODA

ONE MAN'S QUEST
TO END GENDERCIDE IN CHINA

JIM GARROW

THE PINK PAGODA

WND Books
Washington, D.C.

Copyright © James Garrow 2012

Book Designed by Mark Karis

WND Books are distributed to the trade by:
Midpoint Trade Books
27 West 20th Street, Suite 1102
New York, NY 10011

WND Books are available at special discounts for bulk purchases. WND Books, Inc., also publishes books in electronic formats. For more information call (541) 474-1776 or visit www.wndbooks.com.

First Edition

ISBN 13 Digit: 978-1-936488-41-4

Library of Congress information available.

Printed in the United States of America.

DEDICATION

My idol was money.
God showed me His path for me.
I changed.

TABLE OF CONTENTS

Acknowledgments i
Preface iii
Introduction ix

1 My Kingdom for a Child *1*
2 The Cost of One Child *5*
3 Love on Ice *9*
4 Fatz City *13*
5 Walkabout *19*
6 Interview with Bob and Xinyi *25*
7 The Pink Pagoda is Born *35*
8 Luke Skywalker, Meet Yoda *39*
9 Interview with Craig and Kathy *43*
10 Chinese Puzzle *53*
11 Hiding in Plain Sight *59*
12 Rolling Down the River *63*
13 The Great Wailing Wall *67*
14 Crisis of Faith Resolved *71*
15 Is This Your Chinese Baby? *75*
16 To Sleep Perhaps to Dream *79*

17 His Kingdom for a Camaro? *85*

18 The Wild Ride *91*

19 America, Coast to Coast *95*

20 A Canadian Yankee in Hu Jintao's Court *99*

21 Of Tea and Transportation *103*

22 Double Tragedy *109*

23 My Kingdom for a Handkerchief *113*

24 The Good, the Bad, and the Ugly *117*

25 Who is This Guy, Anyway? *123*

26 The Lord Moves in Mysterious Ways *129*

27 Dr. Bethune, I Presume? *133*

28 Bound for Glory *137*

29 Bush Net *141*

30 The Nobel Peace Prize Scandal *145*

31 Dr. James Garrow Doesn't Exist *151*

32 Legacy *155*

ACKNOWLEDGMENTS

This work could not have been achieved were it not for the aid of some pretty exceptional folks. Let me begin by thanking Yoda (not his real name), who was a real godsend and rescued us from ourselves and provided us with safety and security that only someone with supreme *"guanxi"* (connections) could provide. Rest in peace, my friend. To Mr. X and Miss Y, who lost your lives as you attempted to save a little one from evil, accept my humble thank-you and my prayers for your eternal rest.

To my compatriot on the writing journey, Nancy Ellis-Bell, a monstrously large thank-you for your knowledge, strength, and abilities and for pulling the whole thing together. To our folks in China who carry on daily with the task of real "lifesaving," may God continue to richly bless you and your families as you do His work. To World Net Daily for deciding that this story was a "must tell," thank you for putting us out there for the world to read.

To the very significant folks in my past who made such a difference in my life. Mr. Groat, thank you for firing me and teaching me a great lesson at age thirteen. Mr. Groendyke, my social studies teacher at East Kentwood High School in Grand Rapids, Michigan, thank you for telling us that any one of us could change the world. I never forgot that.

To my wife and four children, who always thought that Dad was way out there. You are right; I am, and I love you for just loving me wholeheartedly. To my dad, Robert Garrow, thank you for showing me what loyalty, perseverance, determination, and integrity are all about. To my imperfect Mother, Roberta (Ruby), who said to me a number of times "not to store up regrets"; only now do I realize what that was all about. Thank you for having high expectations for me. I hope I did not disappoint.

For Doug and Marie Sargeant who showed me the balance between "staying the course" and "rejoicing in the Lord" regardless of circumstances, I say thank you. To the God who offers "so great a salvation," I humbly bow. May you be honored through this book.

PREFACE

ONE CHINESE PERSPECTIVE

It was my wife who told me about Jim Garrow and his schools in China and how she had met him in a coffee shop. A phone call to a former colleague in the intelligence service produced some interesting information. Enough for me to know that he had been observed and was considered a friend of China, which was really an indication of some pretty high-level *guanxi*. So I arranged to have an appointment to chat with Dr. Garrow and find out about whether there might be a fit for us to work in a mutually beneficial relationship. Meeting him certainly underscored for me the difference between a typical North American businessperson and this "way out there" visionary. His ideas and presence were quite inspirational and his love of China very profound. I wondered why I had never heard of him before.

Dr. Garrow informed me that he was going to be in my hometown in December of that year and that he wanted to have some special time at the burial crypt of Dr. Norman Bethune. Jim's sense of the spiritual and openness to other people's religious beliefs again showed him not to be your usual North American. I wondered if it was because he was from a Scottish family, raised in Canada and the United States, educated in all of the above, and doing business successfully in my home country that gave him some empathy for the Chinese experience. I couldn't put my finger on it, but it was appealing nonetheless. His visit to the Hall of Heroes and his obvious emotional response to being so close to the remains of Dr. Bethune were almost embarrassing to witness. Not a very "Chinese" response. He shed many tears and was quieter than I would ever see him. There was a sense of reverence that he obviously had for the hero of both Canada and China. I had never seen a white person so emotionally demonstrative before, and yet there was a power in his silence and reverence that I would see again and again in different circumstances. It was here in my hometown that I witnessed for the first time the reaction of a group of Buddhist priests who met him on the sidewalk not far from a school we were visiting. The lead priest stood aside, as did all the other priests as Jim approached. It was like a ship parting waters, and the bows to this *lowai* (foreigner) were totally unexpected. Let me go further and state that whatever went on there and whatever acknowledgment of some special status that they had given Jim, I had never seen priests do before. As he continued on his way, they all had their heads turned to see him walk away. I would witness this same recognition of Jim from total strangers many times as we walked in various cities in the People's Republic.

When my wife and I decided that we would like to go to Canada and see what life would have for us as we approached our retirement from the People's Liberation Army, where we were both career officers, it was not as easy as we hoped it would be. It turned out that I would have to remain a colonel in the intelligence service for five more years until the "Top Secret" knowledge that I possessed would be deemed out-of-date. My specific area of specialty was modeling submarine war strategies against the Americans. I headed up our unit and was responsible for this critical strategic defensive initiative. It was my desire to continue my academic studies in Canada in business administration. This would be at the master's level, and as fate would have it, the University of Western Ontario accepted my credentials and previous degrees and allowed me into the Ivey School of Business. Canada proved to be a great country to move to, and the business degree was another opportunity to hone my intelligence and learn new marketable skills. The real challenge upon graduation was getting a job that would utilize those skills. Far easier said than done. I was not greatly successful in convincing Canadian businesspeople to take a chance on this immigrant with the heavy Chinese accent. But in the education business, many private schools were looking for connections into the Chinese market and seeking Chinese students to come to their Canadian schools. These were students looking to enter universities around the world and using the Ontario Secondary School Diploma as their door opener. This is where I came to chat with Jim Garrow, who was principal of a private school in Toronto with many Chinese students in attendance. I wanted to become an agent for his school and use my connections in China to attract students. He challenged me to show him what I could do in person, in China. He had a unique way of connecting with the students and parents. He was able to give the translators very good information that appealed to what the parents wanted for their children. Hardly anyone who came from China and heard the potential in Jim's descriptions of the school turned down the opportunity to enroll. He is a phenomenal marketer—or is it that he connects with people on an unseen level? After this response to Jim became commonplace, I realized that it was the latter. Somehow this Scottish Canadian educator could communicate with Chinese parents and students in such a way that they wanted what he was offering. His skills in Canada were a mere shadow of what was accomplished in China, and business relationships were sought by many Chinese education entrepreneurs who wanted the "magic" that Jim seemed to bring to the marketing of "international programs."

In China, Jim would capture a school by showing them how to increase enrollment by demonstration. He would approach school officials and ask them to allow him to fill up the empty spaces in their school. He was bold and told them that if they liked what he did, then he expected them to give him a percentage of ownership of the school after he established an international department in the school. Most Chinese school administrators took a show-me stance at his brash boldness. He would almost knock them over with his success and totally out-of-the-box approach to direct marketing a school. I watched him in the city of Yantai go to a large school and tell them that he would fill the spaces and for them to accompany him to a large recreation complex centered in a group of eight thirty-story high-rise buildings. These would house around thirty thousand people with about seven thousand school-aged children in residence. Jim would gather a group of educators situated at tables with marketing materials from the school, and registration forms as well. He would advertise on local Chinese radio an event that would show every Chinese parent whether their school was teaching English properly or not. It was free—bring your children; there would be prizes and contests. Dr. Jim Garrow of the Bethune Institute in Canada would demonstrate for all interested parents and children how easy it was to teach English effectively, and if your children were intelligent and had a good work ethic, they could succeed and enter the best universities in the West if these methods were used. These were bold pronouncements, and the school administrators came, as well as Communist Party officials and parents, to see this braggart fail big-time. But what might have been a flop proved to be a showcase of the talents of the children and the teacher at the front. He enticed them with candy and praised them and laughed with them and taught them skill after skill in front of the gathered throng. Now let's inject some numbers in at this point.

The idea was to come five nights in a row and do the Garrow "English language dog and pony show" to whoever showed up. The first night, with whiteboard set up and PA system fine-tuned to the outdoor environment, twelve children showed up and a straggly group of four or five parents. By the time the hour was over, the noise and excitement had drawn ten more children and about twenty more parents. The invitation was given to come back the next night, and all students and parents were given copious amounts of candy and prizes. What looked to the "officials" to be a failure was deemed to be a "home run" by Garrow. His measuring stick? The hundreds of people on their balconies, watching the spectacle. The PA system ensured that they heard every word in English and translated into Mandarin and Korean. Garrow's final word to the crowd was that on the final night, all who had filled in the registration card would be included in a drawing for five students to get free tuition paid for a full year. Dr. Garrow would do the drawing after the final presentation. He would be available to any parents who would like to meet him after the presentation. Every parent was given a Canadian flag pin for their lapels. About thirty pins were given out that night. When the cars and pickup truck brought the participants back to the school, there was talk of not returning because the evening had been unsuccessful in the eyes of the Chinese school leaders who now proclaimed that they understood the people and that Garrow was entertaining but could not get people signed up in the middle of the year for a new program. Garrow stepped up to the official who was of the highest rank and bet him a month's salary that he would fill the amphitheater (It could hold about two thousand people) and would sign up at least two hundred students by Friday evening. I was getting nervous about this boldness, but I couldn't forget the way people had responded to Jim in Canada. I made a side bet with one of the drivers for a hundred kwai. A number of people wanted to bet against Jim; I took the bets. I got 10 to 1 odds. I stood to lose a thousand renminbi or to make ten thousand. I was a little nervous.

The second night we had a crowd of parents and children waiting for us to unload the whiteboards and PA system, and the addition of video cameras and a TV camera from CCTV, the local cable-TV channel. They had heard that something unusual was happening in the TEDA district (a special economic zone) in Yantai's outer reaches, and they wanted to be there for whatever it was. The name Bethune (pronounced buy-chew-en in Mandarin) was not used in business in China and rarely was the name of some university's medical school or department. It was an honored name, and having the executive director of the Bethune Institute from Canada making presentations on teaching methods for English was actually big news. So day two saw about two hundred kids and about four hundred more people showing up. We had bought lots of stuff, and we lived up to our reputation as a good show. About fifty people signed registration cards and received Canadian flag pins as a result. We got our first two students signed up for the January start of the program (we had no foreign teachers lined up yet—a key promise), and the administrator looked at his colleagues with a surprised look in his eye and his hand in his pocket. He was missing his money already.

Fast-forward to the last night. Yes, every seat was taken for the second day in a row, and our student population for the new program had swelled to more than four hundred students. That was not just a home run; it was a grand slam on a scale never seen before in that city. The secret? Showing parents an excellent and innovative teacher, who showed care for each of the children there and used modern teaching techniques that excited the children. They wanted to come to this program and be taught by foreign teachers, and the parents wanted the doors opened to foreign universities for their children. Their retirements depended on successful children.

I have now spent five years working with the Bethune Institute in

China and Canada and have been constantly reminded that what works is quite simple for children and their parents. Put that future just outside their grasp and they will go for it. Give them a glimpse of what they dream for their children and they will move heaven and earth to attain it. This small description is just talking about schools and education. Pink Pagoda is a whole other universe that I dare not speak about.

COL. JIANG LIU, People's Liberation Army of the People's Republic of China (ret.) and Vice President, Strategic Alliances and Development, The Bethune Institute

(In 2010, Colonel Liu was loaned back to China to head up the team to plan, design, build, and operate the aviation pavilion for the World Expo in Shanghai, PRC. It showcased China's entry into the rather small group of nations capable of producing passenger airliners for international travel and transport. China has arrived. The Bethune Institute is proud of the accomplishments of and the trust placed in our vice president and proud of what the nation of China was able to show the world.)

INTRODUCTION

P lease read this.

I realize that most readers immediately skip over the author's introduction on their way to the "good stuff," i.e., the chapters that unfold the real story.

This is not that kind of introduction.

First of all, it's intentionally short. Just enough information for you, the reader, to quickly peruse and hopefully digest. Just long enough for you to understand why, in order to understand the purpose of my story, you must first understand a little about me and a lot more about China.

I am a very ordinary man. My mother was Jewish; my fathers, Christian. Yes, fathers. I had two: the father I grew up with, and my real father—aka my uncle—whose fatherhood I only discovered this past year. I am a man born out of religious and genealogical contradictions. People tend to either love or hate me. I am not a man of the middle ground.

To my story. From early childhood as a "wee runt of a boy," I determined and succeeded in making lots of money. Not for the sake of being rich, but for the purpose of profound independence. Which is how I came to arrive in China in 1998. I had established a very successful network of colleges throughout Canada, and one contingent of students from China was about to change my life forever.

Originally a Scottish emigrant, I was raised a Canadian, a heritage I am still proud to claim. The heritage I didn't anticipate was China. No, I am not by birth or lineage Chinese. Only my heart and spirit, along with the forty thousand baby girls whose lives we've saved over the past twelve years.

I did not choose to write this book so that people would recognize my name. That was a complete accident. An accident of acknowledgment for a man whose words I admired—Wayne Allyn Root, whose American media appearance prompted me to e-mail him with my kudos for his outspoken, intelligent voice.

That's how it all started. He had/has an agent. He said I should write a book. He said that I should contact her and discuss the possibilities of writing a book. At the same time, many of my friends and colleagues kept telling me that people should know my story. What story? I'm an ordinary man who found himself caught up in extraordinary circumstances who then responded with only one word. Yes.

I did not start out to save the lives of endangered baby girls in China. *Endangered.* A strange word, usually associated with baby seals or dolphins. My passion, my mission, did not start with a major worldview. It all started with one baby girl whose parents were faced with the reality of "setting her aside."

DEATH

Every year, millions of baby girls in China—both in utero and live births—are set aside as a response to China's "one baby" mandate. The Chinese people are not monsters. Their tragedy is that they continue to suffer under a Maoist mandate to control Mao's political enemies, the Han. That mandate was instituted in 1979—about four decades in which to incur huge loss of life.. I do not want to calculate the number of baby girls who have died during that period. I choose to focus on the years between 1999 and the present. Of the millions of baby girls who would have been doomed, Pink Pagoda has saved nearly forty thousand little lives. And more. My organization has helped to redeem the lives of at least eighty thousand parents whose children might have died. That number does not include the extended families. Nor does it include the lives of those children who might have been born from the girls whose lives we've saved.

You should also know that I am considered a criminal by those who consider the work I do to be "human trafficking." I am not a criminal. I am a man willing to be vilified and condemned by those who do not understand China and the profound nature of its ongoing tragedy. When you track Jim Garrow you will find a carefully laid out look which will cause most to write "him" off and give the Pink Pagoda and baby rescues the brush off as the crazed utterings of someone with deep psychological needs. Thank you, Yoda!

The Chinese people are among the noblest in the world. Their culture traverses thousands of years of brilliant minds and significant accomplishments. The Chinese are by no means "inscrutable"; they are scrutable. We in the Western world just need to be able to intelligently scrutinize who they are.

What if, in the North American world, our governments decreed that only male heirs could inherit property from and provide for their parents? What if only one birth certificate were available per family? What if your family was not wealthy and therefore unable to pay the exorbitant waiver to obtain a second or third birth certificate? What would you do?

Maybe you would take a stand, or maybe you would find someone like me. That is why I decided to write this book.

It just takes one person, an ordinary person, to make an extraordinary decision. What happens next is nothing less than the butterfly effect.

I am hoping that my wings will help others loft their wings, to raise up both awareness and action on behalf of all the present and future baby girls of China.

It would be so lovely to see other wings in the sky.

1

MY KINGDOM FOR
A CHILD

I didn't plan to become a criminal. When Xinyi, one of my employees at the Fujing Foreign Language School, where I was principal, was discovered sobbing uncontrollably, I had no idea what my offer to help her "no matter what" would mean—for me personally, for my family, for my schools, and for a baby in deadly peril. Nor could I have known that my decision to help save that one baby would lead to more than forty thousand other babies whose lives I would be instrumental in saving over the next twelve years. One word had launched me on a mission of mercy and incredible danger.

Yes.

The typhoon raging outside my office window on that fateful day, raining one inch per hour without abating, might have tempted me to believe that everything was due to a major tropical depression. No such luck. The storm would eventually fade; not so the torrent of small lives whose very existence would hang upon my lanky frame.

Despite the foul weather, I had been keeping my usual routine, arriving at the school in the early morning hours, before anyone else. I've spent most of my life in schools, from those I attended in Canada, Scotland, and the United States to those I founded in Canada to those I established in China. I especially loved being not only an administrator but also an owner and investor. Today's schedule was no different from any other day's, and I wasn't going to be derailed by a raging storm or a storm of tears.

Ling Mai, another one of my employees, had been the one to tell me about Xinyi's distress.

"Mr. Jim, we don't know what's wrong with her. She's just sitting at her desk, and her whole body is shaking with sobs. We don't know what to do."

I may not have known what to do, but I knew I had to do something.

"I'll find her, Ling Mai; thank you."

I finally found Xinyi at her desk in one of the outer offices. Ling Mai hadn't been exaggerating. Most of the Chinese I worked with were indeed overly demonstrative, and high drama could be expected over the slightest of upsets. Xinyi was in full drama mode.

She was far beyond sobbing; Xinyi was in full wail, her shoulders heaving up and down as great, racking cries came from her small frame. I knelt down beside her and put my arm around her shoulder. The weight of my arm seemed to still her slight frame, but I could feel the sadness running through her like low-voltage electricity.

"Why don't you come with me, Xinyi? We can talk."

When we got to my more private office, I was ready to ask the "right" questions.

"Is it Bob? Is everything all right between you?"

Bob was her husband and one of my best teachers/employees/friend. They made a rather odd couple, he a large man over six feet tall, and Xinyi a petite figure a foot or so shorter. Disparate height aside, they were deeply in love.

Her wordless nod told me the problem wasn't Bob.

"Were you robbed? Did someone hurt you?"

Violence against women was as common in Chongqing as it was anywhere, and we'd had a couple of female teachers who had been groped on their way to work.

She shook her head.

I pulled my chair close to hers and ran through a barrage of more mundane questions. No luck. Finally, her sobs subsided enough for her to speak.

"My sister, she had a baby." Instead of her sounding reassured by such news, the words set off another torrent of tears and sobs.

My mind was trying to quickly distill what the problem with the baby might be. Was the baby sick? Was Xinyi upset because she herself wanted a child and Bob didn't? Had the child been born out of wedlock? I started with what I thought was the most obvious.

"Is the baby okay?"

"Yes, she is—for now."

"Well, that's good news."

But something had alarmed me about the way she emphasized the baby's gender. In stops and starts, Xinyi finally revealed that her sister had called her to inform Xinyi that because of China's "one child policy," her husband wanted to "put the baby aside." At first those words didn't resonate with me at all; when they did, I didn't hesitate in my response.

"Don't worry; we won't let that happen."

Xinyi was not so easily convinced. She stared back at me, all the while pounding her childlike fists against her thighs.

"What can we do? We can't do anything!"

I held her arms, surprised by how easily my hands encircled her tiny wrists.

"This is me you're talking to. There's always a way, and you know I'll find it."

Xinyi heaved an enormous sigh, and I took it as a sign that she trusted me and was surrendering her will to mine.

"Thy will be done; but if there is a way, take this cup away from me . . ."

God's words, not mine; and I remembered them vividly when one of my newborn twin sons, Evan, had almost died the morning he was born. I had begged God to spare his life, to save my newborn son; and in return, I promised I would do whatever He asked of me. The divine request had just arrived.

On a more intellectual, practical level, I had no idea how we were going to proceed. Even for me, the consummate problem solver, this situation was completely beyond my experience. My keen sense of logic kicked in.

The first thing we'd have to do was convince her sister and brother-in-law to hold off on doing anything. Xinyi's sister was opposed to killing her child, but her husband was adamant. He wanted and needed a son.

As Chinese law dictates, only a male heir can inherit family property and also provide for the parents' elder years. Since the establishment of "Mao's Law" in 1979, baby girls had become expendable and China had become a nation awash in grief over having to make such unthinkable choices. I could not allow that to happen to this child.

"Xinyi, tell your sister that I have a business opportunity for her husband. As an honored gift for the opportunity to speak with him, I will wire him fifteen hundred yuan" (about US$250).

The husband already knew who I was, and he would know that I was good for that amount of money.

Xinyi left to make her phone call, and I sat alone to contemplate the choice I had made. China's one-child policy was no longer an urban myth I had heard about offhandedly. Deng Xiaoping's continuation of the Mao policy, instituted to control the Han population, which represented the majority in China, was making me into a revolutionary of sorts. Again. So much of my young life had been focused on upsetting the status quo and challenging authority that had overstepped its boundaries. This time the authority I was about to challenge held the power to not only close my schools but have me killed.

I settled back on my couch and began reviewing some of the more routine paperwork related to my role as administrator. The business math in all these papers was familiar to me, and the numbers predictable. The kind of calculus needed for my new venture was completely new to me and involved human emotion, but it was still within my comfort zone. Irrational, but oddly comfortable.

"Into thy hands . . ."

2

THE COST OF
ONE CHILD

The day for our departure arrived, and a small group of us—including Xinyi, Bob, and myself—headed out for a place known as Hibiscus City, located in the City of Chengdu, the provincial capital of Szechuan. Like Chongqing, it's a thriving, crowded city designated as a commercial zone specializing in telecommunication. I knew of it personally because of my own Internet venture.

We seemed to wind interminably along clogged roads before finally arriving at the Marriott Hotel that would serve as our base of operations. Xinyi immediately got in touch with her sister and set up a time for all of us to meet in two hours. I didn't know what to expect, so I had to surrender some measure of "control" to Xinyi about what I needed to be prepared for. Most important, I needed to know what kind of man I would be negotiating with.

The husband was an engineer with Lenovo, a company that, along with other Fortune 500 companies, had major operations centers here in the city.

"Most important, Mr. Jim, is for you to know that you cannot impress him with your knowledge and experience. If you think that because he comes from the countryside he is naive, you will be misled."

I had no illusion that he might be some kind of bumpkin I could overwhelm with my urban charm or sangfroid. I presumed he would be a worthy "opponent" in our negotiation, and I was ready. What I wasn't necessarily ready for was the high-rise building where the couple lived. While the lobby wasn't as grandiose as some I had seen, it was clear we were not going to be sitting around a proverbial fire discussing simple politics.

We were ushered up into an austerely modern apartment all decorated in dazzling white—from carpets to walls to ceilings to furniture that made me think I was in a contemporary igloo. The igloo had an extraordinary view of the sprawling metropolis below, and it was clear that my negotiations were in no way going to be black-and-white. I knew that I could not simply bargain with this man. Attempting to use financial considerations as a strategy to move him away from his long-held beliefs would not be wise. Like most of the Chinese people I encountered, Xinyi's sister and brother-in-law were Buddhists, and the central seating area where we gathered was dominated by a shrine. Candles were burning and the smell of incense prickled my nostrils, not unpleasantly. Despite those more comforting smells, what I will forever associate with that sad and sweet encounter is the sour smells of simmering cabbage and breast milk.

Like Xinyi, her sister was petite, and her ashen face revealed the ordeal she was going through. To avoid making the baby's presence known to authorities or neighbors, she had given birth at home, and by all accounts the delivery had gone well. But the birth had taken a toll on the mother on an emotional level. With one hand around Xinyi's shoulder, she desperately held the other one close to her empty belly.

In contrast, the father betrayed no emotion and seemed fiercely determined to remain stoic throughout the encounter. Tall and bespectacled, he answered any question posed of him with a steely gaze and slow, deliberate voice. Xinyi was our translator, and shared with us what he was planning to do. He would take the baby to a monastery outside the city and give her to the monks, who would "set her aside." I could barely constrain myself from betraying my horror at the thought of holy men taking a human life. Intellectually, I knew and accepted that I was out of my depth trying to understand Buddhism and all of its precepts; and I certainly knew that many other religions, "in the name of God," were guilty of atrocities against humanity. But infanticide? I was incredulous.

It offered me little or no solace when Xinyi explained that Buddhists, who believe in reincarnation, did not so much see the child as losing one life as they believed it was being "released" to enter another. "What about this life?!" was what I wanted to shout at this man, but I could not. Arguing would gain me nothing, and could potentially contribute to the child losing her life.

The negotiation started slowly, deliberately. At first, he balked at the idea of Xinyi taking the child. He never used the pronouns "my" or "our" when talking about his daughter, and he was obviously concerned that someone might eventually report him to the authorities. The penalty for such a violation was financially severe, and could in some cases be the equivalent of one year's salary. He finally began to soften when we discussed the possibility of an international adoption to either North America or Europe, far away from suspicious minds and paranoia. Each time he seemed to soften in his resolve, he would swing suddenly back to his original plan to end the girl's life. I would counter, promising again to be a man of my word, ensuring him that I would handle everything. Beneath my confident, determined demeanor, I had no idea how I would accomplish that. I just knew I would.

Every time I repeated my promise, he would look over at his wife. She was standing next to Xinyi, her blouse stained both with tears and milk. Occasionally, her infant's cries could be heard from a far bedroom, and she would swoon. The two women looked as if they were in a *tableau vivant*. Too much noise might alert inquisitive neighbors. The negotiation was eviscerating me, but I could not betray any weakness. A child's life was at stake.

I looked first at the husband, seemingly implacable and holding all the power, as is the case with most couples in China, even the more enlightened ones. His wife, on the other hand, stood there in visible agony. She must accept the lesser of two evils: give up her child versus "setting her aside." I had such overpowering sympathy for this woman; I felt no such sympathy for the father. While I could acknowledge that he was up against overwhelming forces, he was in my eyes a coward. Worse, he was willing to be a murderer. How could I sympathize with that?

At one point, tea was served. We all sat around looking exhausted. Bob's primary focus was on his wife, but he offered the right words at the right time to help sustain my focus.

"There is some humanity in him. That's what you have to focus on.

He doesn't want to do this. He needs to."

I nodded, and the negotiations continued.

"Xinyi, tell him that we will set aside money for his daughter, and we'll also help her get an education."

That last bit of information seemed to appease him. He agreed to release the baby into Xinyi's care. He would not have the child killed.

I was too numbed to be elated at the outcome or angry with the man who had been my opponent. The surreal nature of the encounter had overwhelmed me. I just wanted out of the apartment, away from these people, this city. I wanted to be home in Chongqing, safe within my "Western" hotel.

The agony wasn't yet over. We all gathered back in the apartment's central room, and the baby was brought to us. Xinyi's sister suddenly broke free of her husband's grasp and clutched the baby to her. This was more than I could bear. My nerves were raw, but I had to complete what I had started. I held the baby close, her tiny form swaddled in a blanket. She was so light in my arms, and I decided to take the stairs instead of the elevator. I literally trotted down the stairs, my legs weak and my mouth so dry I could not have formed words if I'd wanted to.

Outside, the rain fell on my face, but it was neither a baptism nor an absolution. With huge drops pelting against my whole body, I shielded my tiny bundle from what felt more like the tears of the universe, crying for us all. Back at the hotel, the rest of our entourage would be waiting for us to take care of whatever needs the baby might have. I could hardly wait to throw myself on the bed and collapse. In saving a life, I had taken a life from a grieving mother's arms.

There were no words.

3

LOVE ON ICE

Back home in my penthouse apartment at the hotel—not unusual for successful expats and those doing business in China—the opulence I had grown accustomed to now seemed nearly obscene, a grandiose façade to distract people from the hidden tragedy of the Chinese people.

I looked around my suite, with its polished hardwood floors—marble was common; wood was rare and more prestigious—and carved rosewood furniture. The walls were bedecked with ancient Chinese art, and there were rugs and tapestries in abundance throughout the apartment. From my panoramic windows I looked out onto skyscrapers and the thousands of windows that saw only the prosperity of China. Someday soon I needed to put aside the elegant safety of my chauffeured Mercedes sedan and head out into the city, beyond my comfort zone. For now, I had to bring my head back around to business as usual—more like business as unusual while I reflected on what had just happened in Chengdu.

Inside, the windows rattled in their frames from the new storm raging outside. Another storm was raging inside my head. *What if we had been caught? What could have happened to Xinyi, her sister and brother-in-law? What if something had happened to the baby before we could safely spirit her away? What if, what if?*

Knowing that sleep was impossible, I sat and looked out the windows; the refracting light reminded me of the stained glass windows in all those churches I had attended as a child. My mother, while born a Jew, converted to Christianity, but one of her favorite religious concepts was indeed Jewish—that of *tikkun olam*, a phrase that means "repairing the world." She told me the story of how God had created the world by fashioning glass vessels to hold the Divine Light. When he poured the light into them, they shattered, but a spark was trapped inside each one of the fragments. In that sense, and from the very beginning, the world was a broken place. It was important, she pointed out, that we not despair about the brokenness but focus instead on what we could do to repair the world, to put those broken pieces back together. She also said that each of us had that spark within us, but that our egos and our selfishness prevented us from releasing our own light and doing good in the world. Her words comforted me now, and helped to lessen the pain I could not yet release.

Two days later I was back in my office, caught up in the reassuring mundanity of my daily schedule. Setting up an adoption and providing for the needs of a newborn child seemed an odd counterpoint to that routine, and for the moment I felt secure doing that which I did so well.

"Mr. Jim, can I speak to you for a moment?'

It was Xinyi, and my first thought was that something might be wrong with the baby.

"Sure. Is everything okay with the baby?"

"Oh, yes. We're all looking forward to her adoption, and are so grateful that you found someone so quickly."

"Well then, what is it I can do for you?"

"We have two more babies that need homes."

The thunder outside moved right inside my head. I was temporarily speechless.

"More babies?"

It had been a miracle of fate that I had found a home for the first baby. Craig and his wife, Kathy, he an expat living here in China, had literally dropped into my lap because of a hockey game.

Many of the expats, especially the Canadians, are Zamboni-heads. For those unfamiliar with the game, Zambonis are the machines that maintain the ice for optimal playing conditions. The ice rink I frequented was in one of the largest malls in China, easily dwarfing any of those found in Canada or the U.S. This particular game, like most of those we played, was spirited and at times downright aggressive. One player in particular, a strapping American with reddish-blond hair, slammed into me full force during an offensive move, and down I went. Mostly, there are no grudges in our games, and Craig came up to me afterwards to apologize for his "unnecessary roughness" and offered to buy me a few beers. Tsingtao, of course.

"My name's Craig Allen; sorry about that hit."

"Hey, it's a game. No hard feelings here."

I could tell from his accent that he was from Boston, and it turns out he had played intramural hockey at Harvard. His wife was a teacher back in the States; and as we talked further, he shared that they had not been able to have children, but were hoping to adopt someday.

From my lips to God's ears.

"So, how quickly would you want to adopt a baby?"

I just knew intuitively that he was a solid guy, and the baby would have a good, stable life back in the United States. I put aside the fact that I had no idea how to set up an adoption, or obtain any necessary documents.

"Well, everyone I've talked to here tells me how hard it is, and how long it takes. Kathy and I have gotten rather discouraged."

"So, how quickly would you want to adopt?"

He looked at me oddly, like I had a baby stashed somewhere, but I also knew he trusted me. My reputation in the education world was already widespread.

"I don't know; I'd have to call my wife. Just how soon are you talking about?"

"Right away."

And right away it was. Craig called his wife back home, and in five minutes I had my answer.

"Yes."

At this point, there were no documents to accompany the baby and her new parents back to the United States. Those I would discover in one of the best libraries in the world for doing such research—the local beer house, where expats hang out. It was in one of those pubs that I met my "librarians," who even went so far as to share copies of the documents from their own Chinese adoption process. Paperwork aside, I also learned valuable information about the entire process and what pitfalls to hopefully avoid. I had moved at God's bidding into the adoption business, and I planned to run that business as efficiently as I did my schools. God bless the fool with a big heart.

Xinyi waited for me to respond. She did not look in the least bit worried. To her and the rest of my staff, I was "Mr. Jim, the man who can do anything." Not entirely true, but I was very hard to defeat.

I knew that first of all I was going to have to abandon some of my notions about logical sense. I was also going to have to establish some kind of network to handle everything from paperwork to diapers. It was a surprisingly easy decision. This time, two words.

Tikkun olam.

4

FATZ CITY

Socializing with other expats had been instrumental in my finding a home for our first baby. Hockey rinks aside, it was typically restaurants where I met people who would somehow become part of my Chinese operations, both for schools and my baby-saving organization. Expats, including me, seemed to gravitate towards three restaurants in particular: Rick's Bar, Juggie's, and the truly special Fatz Pizza.

Rick's Bar sat right in the middle of the city, nearest to my school. Many of my teachers liked to hang out there, and we educator-types quickly became a kind of sideshow attraction to the Chinese who liked to hang out with Canadians and Americans. Part of the restaurant was indoors, but the outside patio area was literally right on the street. Chinese passersby would stop and ask to have their picture taken with one or more of us, or they would ask if they could sit down and join us. Most of the Chinese I encountered did not speak English, and I typically had a translator in tow. Those Chinese who did speak a little English loved to practice it on Westerners, and we were always amenable to their request for a little banter.

The second hangout was located in the lower level of a rather dilapidated mall located further out from the center of the city. Juggie's was by any definition a true dive. The walls were painted-over drywall, and whoever painted those walls must have been in a hurry to get the heck out of there.

The floor was cheap linoleum whose curled-up edges looked like old pasta sheets. The tables and chairs were nondescript and mismatched, and the only decoration in the place was provided by the dated musical posters of artists like David Bowie and REO Speedwagon. So why did so many Westerners, and even a handful of curious Chinese, want to hang out there?

Western food and Western conversation. Every expat I've ever met reaches a point of China-overload where what is needed most is to retreat to a place that makes you think you're back in the West. This holds true for both Canadians and Americans. Westerners just need to kick back in a place that serves hamburgers and steaks, and where the conversation can focus around talking openly and honestly about living with the Chinese. In short, talking trash outside the range of Chinese ears. Mind you, with rare exception, all of us really liked the Chinese; it was just an expat thing.

Not that everything Chinese was excluded. Heineken and Tsingtao were still the beers of choice. In truth, they are the same beer with two different names. My personal favorite was Chongqing ale, which came in a one-liter bottle and cost the equivalent of one dollar. My food of choice was the surf and turf, which was, despite the place's decor, actually quite good.

So there we'd all sit and just decompress. The fact that it was a dive didn't really seem to bother anyone. The owners were an Australian and an American, along with a fellow from Hawaii who looked like a native Hawaiian, dressed in his signature Hawaiian shirt. Quite a motley crew, all of us in there, although the motley aspect also included very high-ranking Canadian Embassy officials who seemed right at home in this unseemly dive.

By far, my favorite place was Fatz Pizza, and it was there that my baby-saving persona would encounter an unusual scenario. Fatz Pizza was actually not in Chongqing but in Yantai, up in the northern part of China. Yantai is best known for its major, secret military base—or should I say, supposedly secret—that protects the region right down to Beijing from any attack from South Korea. That placement is highly strategic, and includes Yak fighters and other formidable airplane types, all covered by netting for camouflage.

Yantai itself is a special economic zone where manufacturers like Volkswagen and Audi have plants. The entire region is set up to attract foreigners and foreign business into that economic zone. Again, with food, the region offers up an array of different restaurants, including Fatz Pizza. The owners of Fatz were themselves interesting. The man who started the business is Australian, and when he first came to China, he knew nothing about pizza. When locals started asking for a real pizza place with real pizza, he decided to go to Italy and check out the whole Italian cuisine scene. While there, he met a black Italian classically trained as a chef. The common ground for the two was women. The Australian told the chef that the women in China were the most amazing and beautiful he'd ever seen. That was enough for the chef, and off he went to China.

The building where Fatz was housed was a funny little place. It had three stories—three levels, really, and you entered on the bottom level, which was like a take-out/delivery kind of pizza place. On the second floor was a more formal restaurant that served Italian food. The Chinese don't find it odd for restaurants to have arbitrary divisions or levels, like McDonald's, with its standard-fare space and the more upscale barista environment. On the third floor of this restaurant was the jazz club, which was both a bar and an entertainment destination and included a big floor for dancing. In a word, the place *rocked*.

Expats made it their new favorite place, and so did the top-end Chinese people, who, like the Italian chef, liked to come there for the action and the "babes." I came there for the food and for the Filipino jazz band, whose drummer was especially talented. The band had been touring all over China, but the pay was low, and Fatz became their new, permanent home. Everyone in the band was accomplished, but it was the drummer who really stood out.

He was maybe eighteen or nineteen and had been a pro since he was thirteen. I'm not exaggerating when I say he was a genuine Gene Krupa. He was so outstanding that people would literally stand up close to him while he was playing. You could do that at Fatz, stand a foot away from the performer. I certainly wasn't his only fan. Another admirer turned out to be a link to the second most famous artist in all of China, and I found myself invited to his home nearby.

Given how crowded China's cities are, space is a true sign of wealth and special standing. By strict definition, the artist's place was a ground-floor apartment in a fancy building, but it was unlike any apartment I had ever seen. Although located on the ground floor, it had two stories.

The first level was very, very large, and the second level had an arch that created a dome right in the middle of that second level. Under the dome was his kitchen, not his art collection but his kitchen. In a side room off the kitchen was the equivalent of a steel vault with large cubbyholes like the ones you might see in an old post office. Those slots were thirty-six inches deep, and that's where he stored all of his rolled-up pieces, the ones he had not yet offered for sale. He was not only a prolific artist; he was also a smart businessman. Scarcity equals value and profit, and he was very financially successful. A few years ago there was a major auction held out of California, and the artist's works averaged in the teens of millions each.

The man himself was older and looked a lot like Confucius. He had several young mistresses, and they all attended to his every need. While I was there in his apartment, the women bustled all around him, and it almost felt as if I were back in the old court days of Chinese dynasties.

His artwork was stunning, not what most people might expect of a traditional Chinese artist. His subjects might take their inspiration from ancient stories and characters, but his rendition of those figures was definitely more European. I was mesmerized by his work, and I was completely caught off guard when he offered me a very special book of his artwork. It was one of those special-edition, coffee table–style books that are highly prized by collectors. He simply handed it to me, and it wasn't until I got back to my hotel that I discovered there were several loose-leaf drawings inside the front cover flap. These were some of his sketch sheets in preparation for three of his big works, which later sold in the millions, and here they were, in my hands. I felt as though I were holding the templates for Michelangelo's Sistine Chapel frescoes, and I was awestruck. Why had he given this book and these sketches to me?

I'll never know, because he didn't speak a word of English, and I could in no way fathom one word of his Shandong province dialect, which sounds, even to people from other Chinese provinces, as though the speaker is talking with marbles in his mouth. It's a very old dialect, but clearly art was and is a universal language.

All because of Fatz Pizza and the drummer who invited me to sit in and play drums. I had been a fairly good drummer in high school, and had indicated that to him one night while mesmerized by his playing.

Next thing I knew, he had invited me to join him up on the stage, and being mesmerized quickly turned to being profoundly embarrassed. Thank goodness the place was fairly empty that night, but it did hold one very significant patron, the son of that famous artist. The drummer introduced me as the "adoption guy I told you about," and I was not only on my way to meeting the famous artist; I was also on my way to another adoption.

When I left the club that night, the son climbed into the cab with me, and the word "baby" wasn't long in coming.

He and his wife had tried unsuccessfully to have children of their own, and they desperately wanted to adopt. The drummer had mentioned this "Garrow guy," and here I was, about to play a different instrument.

"Sure, I can help you."

His gratitude came in the form of an invitation to meet his father; mine, in the form of a baby. Fatz Pizza hadn't only satisfied my hunger and need for good entertainment; it had led me to a Chinese master and a new Chinese father.

"Turn it on, turn it on again."

"Turn It On Again," by Tony Banks, Phil Collins, and Mike Rutherford, recorded Autumn 1979, by Genesis, on Duke. Charisma Records; Atlantic (U.S. & Canada), 7"and 12" (vinyl).

5

WALKABOUT

When the current storm finally cleared, I decided it was time for my foray out into the "other" China. My excuse for abandoning my car and driver was that I wanted to see if I could find my way to my favorite tailor's shop, where my shirts were made.

First, I made sure to put all my necessary papers and money into specific pockets in my signature Tilley vest. I always wore vests with an array of pockets, and I was known for those as much as for my long hair. Before leaving I decided to have one more cup of coffee, and managed to spill it on my vest. I quickly changed into another, completely oblivious to the fact that I had left out the all-important taxi card, which could tell anyone which hotel I was staying in. Not that I planned on getting lost. I had watched my driver navigate highways ranging in size from major arteries to dirt-packed roads. I have an excellent sense of direction, and I was looking forward to discovering Chinese life beyond the Marriott.

Each penthouse floor has its own concierge, and the one on my floor cordially asked if I would like him to summon my driver.

"No, thank you. I'm going to walk."

"Oh no, sir; that would not be advisable."

The concierge was doing his job, and I thanked him accordingly for doing it well.

Down in the massive lobby, with its huge, carved lions and pillars reaching skyward to the penthouse floors, I maneuvered past the stands of lush greenery and headed for the lobby doors.

"Dr. Garrow, shall we call your car for you?"

Again, with courteous solicitations.

"No, thank you; I just want to walk. Don't worry; I'll be okay."

The staff continued to insist, but out I went into the mean streets of Chongqing. Outside was the major, six-lane highway. Once I crossed that, the roads continued to get smaller and more narrow until I finally reached the rural area where my tailor was located.

The road looked surprisingly different on foot, and how silly that it hadn't occurred to me that all the street signs would be in Chinese. Landmarks that I thought I would remember were not so apparent when on foot. It wasn't that I was afraid; I wasn't. While I knew that pickpockets were not uncommon, I also knew that my ever-expanding guanxi would protect me. The worst possibility were beggars, and I could kindly put them off.

Here where the streets had only two lanes and were mostly dirt packed, I saw many "shanties" built into the sides of hills, one seemingly stacked upon the other. Everything had been salvaged, from bricks to tin to cardboard to tin and paper. Even the windows were salvaged and fitted awkwardly into the walls. Recovered bricks were the most prized building material, but not as common as the other materials. What we might call garbage in North America was carefully scavenged and piled up as high as twenty feet on precariously balanced bicycles. The biblical concept of gleaning was highly respected in China. There were no official garbage collectors, and refuse dumped into the street was quickly recovered and stacked upon queues of bicycles. It would have been unenlightened, even dangerous, for a well-meaning foreigner to offer money to such "beggars." Small as it might be, there was a place for these people in the social system.

There is, of course, a harsh side to such a system. There are no social services that would provide "welfare" in China. If a person has no food, he starves to death. Even near five-star hotels in the more affluent parts of the city, it wasn't unusual to see an emaciated body lying in the road. People would simply step over the body until some official called for its removal. The only salvage value for such a wretched soul was in reincarnation.

As I walked along these poor streets, I waved and smiled at everyone I encountered. Despite their poverty, everyone I met was clean. Even the community toilets shared by so many were always kept in sanitary condition.

Moving now from these residential neighborhoods into the more commercial areas, the streets were lined with little shops that obviously shuttered down at night, much like the ones you might see in New York City. Bustling with activity, a shop selling grotesque animal parts shared a common wall with an auto repair shop, which shared a common wall with an apothecary, which shared a common wall with a clothing store. There was no sense of commercial order in any of this. On the other side of the street was a pool hall, filled with men wielding pool cues and smoking cigarettes. Cigarette smoke was everywhere, which only added to the pollution already choking the air. In many of China's cities, the particulate matter caused by coal-burning generator plants is at a level of 140 parts per million. Compare this to a city like New York, where the ppm count is 23. Chinese city dwellers were choking and coughing to a degree that almost defied belief. Urine and feces were also present; although I did have to marvel at what I have come to call "the whistle stop." Toddlers barely able to walk would, on a whistle command from their mothers, stop and urinate on the spot. Clad only in T-shirts, there were no diapers or pants to interfere with their whistle stop.

In addition to the stench, there were also the constant crowds, making me feel as though I had been pressed into a living, fast-moving current. Some of the poor were dressed in Western clothes, others in more traditional garb, and some of the older ones still wore their Mao-inspired garments—signature jacket and navy blue cap with red star.

There I was, among the ranks of the poor, lost but in no way afraid. I knew that at some point someone would find me. Find me they would have to; I had also left behind my cell phone. I was truly cut off from all communication with my familiar world.

"Marriott Hotel? Marriott Hotel?"

No one spoke English, and it was silly, of course, to think that the poor would have any concept of a luxurious hotel. Nonetheless, it must be some kind of North American thing to simply repeat oneself, just more loudly.

"Marriott Hotel? Marriott Hotel?"

Curious people smiled at me with discolored teeth—or no teeth. Their smiles were no less beautiful.

Finally, an inspiration. "And a little child shall lead them . . ."

I would enlist the help of children, soon to be getting out of school, to help me back to civilization. Sure enough, along came a boy around ten years old on his bicycle. Seeing a foreigner, known in Chinese as *lowai*, in this part of the city was enough to make him stop and investigate. He did speak a few words of English, but was on his way to a violin lesson and couldn't stay to help me. At least I think it was a violin lesson, given how he described with his hands what I thought looked like someone playing a violin. That, or he was telling me, "Too bad, so sad" as he rode off.

Eventually, more children began to gather around, one as young as four and the rest ranging upward to around ten. I was now being led, to where I didn't know, by seven curious children with foreign prize in tow.

I remembered that there was a McDonald's back on the major highway. Perhaps they would know how to get me there. The restaurant manager would surely speak English, and I'd be back on my way to the hotel. There was no hope of a taxi in this area, so it had to be the Golden Arches.

"McDonald's?"

I had gone from dirt streets to pay dirt.

Their faces lit up, and in broken English they told me that they knew where McDonald's was. For once, I was looking forward to fast food. The route to reach our destination was not nearly so fast. Up and down narrow alleys, off onto various side streets, the word must have gotten out that they were with a foreigner with money, and our ranks began to grow. Ultimately, we arrived at McDonald's, fifteen children strong. The restaurant manager did not look especially pleased to see us.

The white-gloved gatekeeper greeted us at the door, and as she stared suspiciously at the boisterous group of children surrounding me, she asked in perfect English,

"How can I help you?"

I responded with the universal language: money. In China the currency is called *renminbi*. The slang expression is *kwai*. Think dollars and bucks. I handed her the equivalent of $140.00 to cover the cost of whatever the children wanted to eat. That $140.00 was equivalent to one month's salary for the manager, and she knew that she could expect a very large tip for putting up with this ragtag group.

Now we were welcomed inside the Golden Arches, and in the children rushed. In China there are only five items on the daytime menu: the Big Mac, fish sandwich, chicken sandwich, french fries, and chicken nuggets. There is also a small breakfast menu, but chicken nuggets are far and away the Chinese favorite. Not so, mine. The nuggets are made from dark chicken meat, and even the rest of the meat selections just don't taste right to me. While the children ordered their feast of a lifetime, I made my way through an open alcove into the upscale coffee shop, a standard feature in every large McDonald's. This restaurant could easily accommodate three hundred people or more, and I was happy to make my way ever so briefly to the other side. The attendants there and in the main restaurant all wore white gloves, and patrons never cleared their own tables. Like the scavengers who collect garbage from the streets, these white-gloved attendants dutifully collected any refuse left behind.

In contrast to the more low-scale furnishings of the main restaurant, the coffee shop is outfitted with comfortable leather chairs, art-bedecked walls, fancy coffee drinks, and pastries. Patrons from the "other side" are not allowed in. Being a foreigner and white, I was allowed in. After purchasing my mochaccino and a danish, I headed back across the divide to join my little group.

There we all sat, children on my lap, children with their arms around me, and mine around them. We were just one big family enjoying a Happy Meal. I suspected that most of these children were having their first-ever hamburger, and I didn't feel particularly hurried to get back to my hotel. We had our own special table, and the manager explained to everyone within earshot that I was "Jiānádà" (a Canadian). It was an expression of honor, unlike the word *Megwa*, reserved for Americans.

After about an hour the taxi arrived, and I left behind the smiles of satisfied children and a well-tipped manager. The taxi driver in his spotlessly clean VW Jetta also wore white gloves. The children were all jumping up and down and waving as I drove off, and for once I really hadn't minded fast food. In some ways, the restaurant felt more like a desperate anchor to my North American roots. I sank down into the seat, watching one part of the city disappear while a more familiar one emerged.

Where I had been, there were no crystal chandeliers or huge, carved lions or fountains with bridges and koi. The people seemed no less happy than the ones toddling about on marble floors. As we drove up the fifty-yard-long driveway to the hotel, I reminded myself that empty space was the ultimate sign of wealth. "Ching an" is a familiar expression in China, and refers to the value of clear space. I was now approaching my own sense of clear space.

Even before we reached the lobby entrance, I could see guards at the top of the driveway, frantically using their walkie-talkies, letting the staff know that I was back safely. When I stepped out of the taxi, I was assailed by members of the hotel staff, who were all breathing a collective sigh of relief.

"Dr. Garrow, everyone was so worried about you. Please, please, don't do that again!"

I apologized and made my way back through the lobby and past all the lush greenery and sentinel lions. I felt no need to rush, so common for Westerners in China. Even my heart felt more open than it ever had before. I never did find the shirt I was looking for, but I found something else that I would wear forever.

Peace.

6

INTERVIEW WITH BOB AND XINYI

It wasn't always peaceful on either the school or baby-saving front. Mostly, my employees were professional, accomplished, and easy to work with. One of them, however, was a perennial thorn in my side. Now that I had begun rescuing babies, in addition to my school functions, this particular teacher had begun to pose a more sinister problem. We'll just call him Steve.

Unlike the rest of my teaching staff, whose generous living stipend allowed them to live comfortably in well-outfitted apartments or houses, Steve had chosen to live among Chinese teachers in a poorer section of the city, where the monthly rent was only a hundred dollars. I didn't mind his frugality; if he wanted to save money for his eventual return to the United States, I had no issue with that. My issue was with his profound lack of physical hygiene and his teaching abilities, which were not at all up to my performance standards. Unfortunately, I had inherited him when I took over the school where he was teaching. Firing him would have been awkward, so I, along with the rest of the staff, tried our best to tolerate him.

It wasn't easy. He had a mean-spirited demeanor, and seemed determined to cause me grief. To put a fine point on the matter, he didn't like me one bit and behaved as if he was on a mission to uncover some nasty truth about me and my schools. Most recently, he had been badgering Bob and Xinyi because he knew that the three of us were very close, and that they were somehow involved in my baby-saving operations. He had only heard snippets of information about babies being adopted, but I had growing concerns that his motives with Bob and Xinyi might be more insidious.

In the first place, it was well known by everyone around him that Steve didn't especially like the Chinese people, and that his only motivation for coming to China as a teacher was to earn more money than he could back in the United States. That greatly offended me, because all of the teachers I had personally hired truly embraced both the country and its people. If Steve were some kind of mole, whom might he be working for? That can of worms had nearly limitless possibilities, so I wasn't quite sure which course of action to take.

Meanwhile, Bob and Xinyi were increasingly distressed by Steve's persistent questions, and finally had come to me asking how best to handle the situation. If they dismissed him entirely, it would just fuel his rude curiosity or darker motives. We needed to take assertive action, but what? Fortunately, we had one important thing in our favor.

Steve was stupid. Irretrievably, hopelessly stupid.

Together, Bob, Xinyi and I hatched a plan to end this situation once and for all. We decided to set up a "mock" interview with Bob and Xinyi. They would agree to answer Steve's questions once and for all, and Steve would have to agree that those answers would be the end of the issue. I would function as the moderator, and keep everything focused and on track. Bob and Xinyi agreed, and I put in a call to Steve.

"Hi, Steve. Dr. Garrow here. Listen, you know that I like my schools to run smoothly, and I also respect that you have some questions which we need to address. I've come up with a way to resolve this once and for all. Are you interested?"

There was a slight hesitation on the other end of the line. I guessed the pause was due to Steve's disbelief that I was willing to entertain his request.

"Well, uh, sure, Dr. Garrow. You know, I just don't want any of us to be placed in any kind of jeopardy; and, well, it just seems like Bob and Xinyi are the closest ones to you. Really, I didn't mean to offend you or anything."

I knew his words were hollow, but hey, so was he.

"Okay, then, here's the plan."

I then carefully detailed how the "interview" would be conducted.

He would have to send me a short list of questions, no more than seven or eight, and I would review them. Then he and I would agree on the wording for those questions. Once the question was asked, he wouldn't be allowed to interrupt. If I felt there needed to be some kind of clarification, or if Bob and/or Xinyi needed any qualification, then I would be the facilitator. Once the interview was over, that was it. Steve had to agree never to bring up the matter again.

I also had another motivation for setting up this interview, and I did not share that with Bob and Xinyi. What I ultimately wanted was to terminate Steve's employment, and this interview could later be used against him for not being a "team player" in our schools. I really don't like such machinations, but with Steve, Machiavelli was my new best friend. At the very least, we had to defuse Steve. Beyond that, termination was definitely my goal.

Steve agreed to my terms, and I consulted with Bob and Xinyi about the best date to conduct our interview. We chose the date, and then discussed some of the parameters for the discussion. I also told them that we would receive the questions in advance, and that they wouldn't have to worry about being caught off guard. We were set.

The questions arrived from Steve, and I was both shocked and surprised. Remember "stupid"? I couldn't have formulated better questions to serve my purposes. I sent back a few minor wording changes, and we were good to go.

The day for the interview arrived, and the phone conference arrangements were all in place. Bob, Xinyi, and I sat in our conference room, while Steve hunkered down in his little apartment. I knew that his favorite haunts were those rather seedy karaoke bars throughout the city, places where the drinks were served by bare-breasted women whose other services required an additional bar tab. Even though I knew we'd be calling him in his apartment, I couldn't get rid of that image of him, in his slovenly clothes and leering face, ogling the unfortunate women who had to work in such places. I didn't share that image with Bob and Xinyi. Even for me, that would have been über-imp.

"All right, everybody; we're ready to start. Steve, go ahead and ask your first question. Also, I know we discussed it before, but I'm just affirming for the group that I am taping this interview. We all understand that, yes?"

A round of yeses, and Steve was ready to launch his first question. I reminded everyone as well that depending on the question, either both Bob and Xinyi could answer, or just one of them. Steve acknowledged that, and it was time to start.

"Hi, guys; I want to say first that I really appreciate your doing this. You know, I just want some things to get cleared up."

"We understand, Steve." Bob's voice may have had a flat register, but his face was anything but flat. Bob is a no-bullshit kind of guy, and that's the only way to put it. When he had first attended one of my teaching seminars back in Canada, he had made it a point to come up to me afterward and tell me in those exact words that my presentation was the first one he had attended that wasn't b.s. I took it as an honest compliment, and that's how we began our relationship as educators for a common purpose.

"Okay, first question. How would you describe your experience working with Jim both as an educator and as the man who saves babies?"

Since the three of us had already seen the question, no jaws dropped, and Bob didn't miss a beat.

"I was pretty jaundiced with most of the educators I had seen do presentations on classroom management and organization, but Jim was totally different. He was clear, he made sense, and I could tell right away that this was a guy who did what he said he would do. I also noticed that others in that presentation were very moved by his presence. That was the first time I saw for myself that this was a man who had a special gift for getting things done, and getting others to help him whenever he needed help. In a word, I *trusted* him. Still do. When he offered to help Xinyi with her sister's baby, I had no doubt that he would figure a way to make that happen. And he did. When a couple of other people approached him with babies needing adoption, Jim figured out all the details. Nobody was compromised; nobody was in danger. That's Jim; that's how he does things."

I had to interject one thought.

"We're a team, Steve, whether it's the educators in my schools or the people involved in helping with baby girls. You already know that I'm willing to put my head on the chopping block for my principles. The secret is eliminating the chopping block."

"Yes, yes." It was Xinyi this time.

"I was so upset over my sister's situation, and I had no idea what to do. When Dr. Jim got involved, I became calm. That is his gift."

"And I need to add in, Steve, that when Jim called me back in Canada and asked me to come teach in one of his schools here in China, I jumped at the chance. He remembered me, and I remembered him. I said yes without a moment's hesitation," said Bob.

"Well, it sounds like you two are totally happy working with Jim, and that you trust him all the way."

For Steve, it probably wasn't the kind of response he might have hoped for, but I was smiling all the way, offering a wink and a nod to Bob and Xinyi.

Bob couldn't resist one more comment.

"You know, Steve, it's almost like Jim is guided by some force, divine or whatever, that's much bigger than all of us. Everyone feels safe around him because they can sense that."

Steve didn't respond, but I could almost imagine him running his fingers through his dirty hair. I don't think there was a spiritual fiber in his whole body.

"I'll take that one step further."

Xinyi was leaning across the table, almost as if she wanted to put her tiny hands around Steve's throat and throttle him into awareness.

"I personally believe that Dr. Jim is the reincarnation of a saint, maybe Dr. Bethune, and I'm not alone in that belief. The Chinese people who come in contact with him believe that too. Even people who haven't met him but who have heard about him speak his name with genuine reverence."

Steve couldn't resist tossing in a new question.

"But he fired you, Xinyi. How does that measure up with everything you just said?"

Xinyi gestured to me that she wanted to answer his question, so I kept quiet.

"He had to fire me. Dr. Jim has a firm rule about office romances, and Bob and I had broken that rule. It was a matter of integrity. Dr. Jim could not exempt me from that rule, and I totally accepted his decision to fire me."

Now it was Bob leaning across the table, wanting to add more.

"Listen, Steve, what you don't know is that Jim sent Xinyi lots of tutoring business after he fired her, and she ended up making more money than when she worked for him. He did the right thing, and the universe took care of the rest."

"Yeah, sure. Well, let's move on to the second question. What is it about the Chinese culture and people that appeals to you, Bob?"

God only knows what Steve hoped to find out from Bob, but Bob couldn't have been more blunt.

"At first, when I came here to China, nothing. Absolutely nothing. But that wasn't because of China or anything here. I was running away from Canada and from a failed relationship. It took me a while to realize what a gift China and Jim's invitation were in my life. Everyone knows that I'm kind of a hyperactive sort of guy, and mouthy. China helped me become more of what Xinyi calls a "gentle giant." China got into my soul, and I've even come to believe that I've lived here before in a previous life."

At this point, I could only imagine Steve grabbing a fistful of his hair in pure, incredulous disbelief. "What? Like these rude little people? He must be kidding!"

It was a perfect moment.

Xinyi only made it better.

"You know, Steve, I would have moved back to Canada with Bob. I was willing to give up the China I love in order to be with the man I love. It was Bob who brought me back more firmly into my 'Chinese-ness,' if there is such a word."

Those words were ironic and portentous. When Bob died several years later, it was Xinyi who requested that I bury his ashes back in Canada, on his home soil, where I could visit him. I was so deeply honored to receive the beautiful lacquered box tied with a saffron ribbon. I did scatter those ashes, but that beautiful box has a permanent place in my home.

"How did you meet Xinyi, Bob?"

His voice sounded like someone caught in very uncomfortable territory who wanted back to simple black and white.

"At the beginning, and even though everyone knows she's beautiful, it was the fact that she spoke English that got us started. I had someone to talk with. The more time I spent with her, the more I saw myself becoming a better, calmer person. She wasn't deferential in the way that some people think Chinese women are towards men, or their husbands. Yes, she was very accommodating, but never servile. That's one of the things I loved about her. She embraced her Chinese heritage, but she was also her own woman. Hell, she had to go up against her own father to allow the marriage. What can I say? She won."

Again, I saw clenched fingers wrapped around greasy hair, completely oblivious to the Chinese puzzle box he had entered.

"You mean that neither one of you had concerns about saving babies? I mean, come on; it's illegal. You could have been arrested or killed, and what about other people helping you?"

There was the question he had been wanting to ask all along. Bob picked up the gauntlet.

"At first, there was no time to think about danger. We just did what had to be done. We didn't know how Jim was going to do it, but we knew that he would, and that whatever had to be done would be done right."

More clenched fingers, and then Xinyi came in with another homerun.

"I just thought that my prayers, and those of other suffering mothers, had been answered."

"I knew that I was part of something so much bigger than myself, and I was honored by that."

Bob's words were a perfect complement to Xinyi's.

Steve was swinging away with a rubber bat. He needed new leverage, so in came another new question.

"So, Jim, is there anything about your baby-saving program that you would change?"

I'm a master at left field hits, and I caught that fly ball before it could slam into my face.

"For the most part, no; but then even if I wanted to, I couldn't share any of those changes, for obvious security reasons."

Bob and Xinyi smiled at me from across the table.

"All right, one more question."

I was looking down at Steve's original list of questions, and there were still five to go. Or not.

"How has being involved with saving babies changed both of your lives?"

This question was on the list, but the tone in Steve's voice told me it was more of a concession to having not gotten the kind of "dirt" he had hoped to find. Bob went first.

"I know that I'm part of a greater purpose, that my life is not just about being an educator, being a husband, being friends with good people like Jim; this is about fate, my fate, and the fates of all those little babies whose lives we save. I am forever changed by this, and I am grateful to Jim for honoring me as part of his team."

"Steve, this is our divine mission, Bob's and mine, Jim's, everyone who helps to save babies," Xinyi added. "We are all blessed."

There was a brief moment where no one spoke, and then Steve brought it all to a close.

"Okay, well I guess that takes care of what I wanted to know."

He was defeated, and he knew it. We weren't gloating, just relieved that this exercise in futility was over. Not that the interview hadn't been useful; we had probably succeeded in defusing whatever plan Steve had in mind. It was more about having to deal with a base human being whose stupidity was pandemic in a world where stupid, cruel laws create the need for people like me and Bob and Xinyi and Pink Pagoda to intervene.

Bob and Xinyi looked relieved that it was over, and I suggested that we all head out for a couple of beers to relax a bit. For Steve, there would be no sigh of relief or vindication.

I pictured a nearly bald little man, more of a real dwarf than Yoda. A striking contrast to the towering hulk of Bob, who was a giant in more ways than one. He enriched not only Xinyi's life, but mine as well. Sadly, his life ended far too soon. It wasn't very long after our mock interview that I got a call from Xinyi in that frenzied voice I recognized all too well.

"Mr. Jim, Mr. Jim!"

The rest of her words disappeared into sobs, and I had to ask her to repeat what she was saying. I thought at first the garbled words might be the result of her calling from Macau, where she and Bob were vacationing in order to catch the Grand Prix race taking place there. Her call, as it turned out, was actually coming from Shenzhen, where the high-speed hydrofoil had just returned them from the island to the mainland. It appeared when they arrived that Bob was sleeping in the bottom of the boat, and no one had taken any special notice of him. Once at the dock, it quickly became clear that he was not asleep. He was dead.

"Bob's gone; he's gone!"

A chill went up my spine when I began to realize what she was saying.

"Xinyi, it's okay; just calm down a little bit and tell me what happened. I'll take care of whatever I have to do."

She managed to gulp down her sobs, and told me in a very controlled but shaky voice what had happened. Apparently, he had just decided to take a nap, and no one paid any attention after that. Xinyi had been topside, talking to the other passengers, and only when it was time to disembark did everyone realize that he had died, from causes unknown, during the trip. Later, it was presumed to have been a sudden heart attack, but Xinyi didn't want an autopsy. I fully agreed with her.

"Don't worry, Xinyi, I'll take care of everything."

For a moment, I was back in my office at school, my arms around her, and then my hands holding her tiny wrists. Of course I would take care of everything. That's what I do. Then, it was all about saving a baby; now it would be about saving her from any unnecessary pain.

Once she returned to Chongqing, we sat down to discuss the funeral arrangements. Bob had already been cremated, for which I had gladly paid the cost, and now I wanted to know what kind of arrangements she wanted me to make.

"I want him to go home, to Canada. I think he would want to be with his family, in his own country."

Now the tears were mine. I knew how much she loved him, and what a tremendous sacrifice it was for her to give up his cherished remains. Pure, beautiful Xinyi.

"Of course, Xinyi; whatever you want."

Now came a journey of nearly Grand Guignol proportions. After celebrating Bob's life in a Buddhist service there in China with a couple hundred high school students whose lives he had so profoundly touched, and the sister of Hu Jintao in attendance, I gave Bob's daughter in Canada a call. She was going to arrange for a service back there, and I offered to bring Bob home. In a wheely bag.

Xinyi had placed his remains in a container, which I had not yet seen, into one of those wheel-on bags that many travelers use. When I arrived in Canada, I managed to get through customs, but then had to make my way through a terrible snowstorm before arriving at the site where the services were being held. The hall was festooned with pictures of Bob depicting not only his professional life, but every possible aspect of who he was. Very impressive. In the middle of the hall was a dais where his ashes would be set, and I rolled the bag up to it. I could not have been more surprised or impressed.

There, intricately wrapped in saffron cloth, was a box I could not yet see. I undid the unusual knot, and the cloth fell away in the shape of a lotus, as if it had been arranged to do so. Sitting there atop the cloth was this amazing box. It was rectangular, intricately carved, and there on one side was an oval inset with a picture of Bob in it. The people in the room, including me, nearly gasped. Such beauty for a beautiful soul.

I was in the third group of speakers who shared all manner of stories about Bob during the course of the celebration, and the wine flowed freely, along with the tears and smiles. I had only one regret.

Xinyi should have been here.

7

THE PINK PAGODA
IS BORN

After the first baby, word spread quickly. Within a very few weeks we were fully invested in the baby adoption business. I also became vastly aware of how expensive this was going to be. From the beginning, I was spending my own money; and while I was indeed willing to do whatever it took to save babies, I could see that the money pit would only continue to get deeper and bigger. Furthermore, my associates saw no limits on the help I could provide. They had seen what I accomplished with my schools; and I was not just an employer, I was family. That is true throughout China. Employers have and accept responsibility for their employees, just as a benevolent father would do. It's much like the scene in the 1962 movie *Lawrence of Arabia*, where Anthony Quinn describes the relationship with those under his governance.

*"I am a river to my people."**

The Chinese see things much the same way. Employers, people in power, are a river of blessings to their people. When one of my people would come in and say, "We have a baby to save right now," it never

---

*Lawrence of Arabia, *screenplay by Robert Bolt and Michael Wilson; dir., David Lean; prod. Sam Spiegel. Horizon Pictures; distributed by Columbia Pictures, 1962.*

occurred to that person that I would say anything other than yes. After taking a few moments in solitude to finish my tea, I would call the employee back in and ask for all the details. Not only was I a river to my people; I was in the river.

That river was fraught with dangerous currents. As a foreigner, especially, if I were caught "stealing babies," as the Chinese authorities would perceive my actions, I would be killed. Pure and simple. The aftermath of my death would be the dismantling of my educational network in China, and hundreds of employees would be left with no means of support. Failure was not an option.

People have often asked how I dealt with that kind of pressure. Simple: I didn't. If I had put my conscious attention on eventualities, I would have been thwarted in all my efforts. I just pressed on. I also reminded myself of the promise I had made to God those many years ago. I was connected to a kind of divine certainty, and I embraced what for many is simply an evangelical cliché—"Let go and let God." For me it was not a cliché, but a mandate. That said, it wasn't as if I felt weighted down by my choices. Quite the contrary, I felt more like *Mad* magazine's Alfred E. Newman.

"What—me, worry?"

I have always had a "different" brand of humor, and most people consider me very funny—in a good way. We are surrounded by cosmic jokes and mishaps. Being overly serious accomplishes nothing but produces more fodder for the Western medical profession. When I realized that we would have to provide wet nurses for the newborns we were saving, wet nurses somehow appeared. When the need for diapers was clearly imminent and constant, I arranged to have a North American company use their empty cargo containers bound on a return trip to China for diaper transportation. That was also the way I managed to get formula into the country, which was then made available from a local apothecary. Another cliché was for me just a way of doing things. "Where there's a will, there's a way."

Guanxi also played an important role in my getting what I needed. A water purification system was essential, and that was proving much more difficult to obtain. To my rescue came a military official whom I had helped with an adoption, and in short shrift I was gifted with the kind of system used by the military. No explanations were needed or offered. I knew that the explanation was baby number five.

In those first two-and-a-half years of Pink Pagoda operation, which got its name later in the game—*pagoda* for a safe haven and *pink* for girls— we saved three thousand babies with an operational network of roughly forty people spread across several provinces. One of the most challenging aspects of the program was my own sense of being a colossus between two worlds. When I would return home to Canada to be with my family, part of me was still in China. In China, there was that constant tug of my wife and children, who were sacrificing so much for me to be able to pursue my calling, my mission. We did talk on the phone every day, but our physical separations lasted months at a time. There was, of course, a certain kind of humor when I did come back to Canada.

"Oh, the emperor's here. I wonder how long he'll be around."

Not sarcastic, just a humorous acceptance of what I was doing. It's not that I didn't need to be somehow "retrained" for life as Jim, the guy from Guelph. Back in China, I cut a major figure with my posh penthouse, Mercedes sedan, chauffeur, and money that I could spend as I chose. That ability to spend and transfer money was tied to my special red-and-gold foreign experts license, a document rarely accorded someone who wasn't Chinese. Not only does that gold-embossed "passport" allow one to move money about without restrictions; it also protects the bearer from any kind of harassment at airports and the like. That document was always tucked into one of the pockets in my signature Tilley vest; that is still true here in Canada. I never leave home without it. One might be curious how I managed to get such a document. Think back to 2000, and that special student in my class at Shaw College in Canada. That special student is the one who invited me to come to China the first time, and who introduced me to the inner circles of connected, powerful people, including her uncle, Hu Jintao. No more needs to be said.

Nonetheless, I was a foreigner, and I stuck out like that proverbial sore thumb. I knew that with every adoption I was being watched by someone, somewhere. I just didn't know who. I also didn't know if I might be arrested. Again, if I had focused on contingencies, I would have been immobilized by fear. As I remember hearing once, "I eat fear for breakfast." In my case, I had it along with my coffee.

Mostly, I wasn't directly involved in the transfer of a child. I was simply the money man. One adoption required that I be present at the exchange, and I will never forget that wild chase.

Our initial preparations offered no indication of any problems. We arrived at the baby's home, collected the child, and headed back to our car. There were three of us, two women and me, and all seemed to have gone well until we headed out on the road. All too quickly, we noticed that we were being followed, and the game plan would have to change. We headed instead for the subway, and quickly hatched a bait-and-switch maneuver. One woman would be holding the baby, the other a baby "bundle." Once on the subway, the two women split up, and our pursuers had no way of knowing which woman had the baby they were after. The woman with the real baby got off at the designated place, and rejoined us on our journey back to Chongqing. It was the closest call we'd had so far, but sadly, it was not to be the last or the most dangerous.

That danger was moving in all around us, but like the Buddhist koan about the fish who doesn't know it's in the water, I didn't know that I was starting to drown. Time for a benevolent fisherman.

8

LUKE SKYWALKER, MEET YODA

I never knew from one minute to the next who might come through my office door. Every time I looked up from my desk to see who was there, it could as easily be a student, an employee, or someone needing a home for a baby. I just stayed focused on "Yes."

The day of my life-changing visit had been so busy that I hadn't even had time to get to my favorite coffee shop in time for breakfast. It was nearly noon, and I couldn't handle any more slogging through paperwork, so off I went in search of my special coffee and favorite table.

In 2002, as was and still is traditional with most Chinese people, the drink of choice was tea. I preferred coffee, but not just any coffee. It had to be Tim Hortons, a famous Canadian producer, and I liked it brewed in a very special way. Few people ordered it this way because of the cost. Fifteen dollars for a carafe of coffee was exorbitant, but I loved the quality of the brew, which had to be specially prepared at my table in what looked like a Bunsen burner and a hookah. Whenever I ordered it, people around the restaurant would all stare at the ceremony of careful preparation and the copious volume of steam. It truly served to ground me, and I don't mean that in an ironic way.

The restaurant itself was rather elegant, and furnished IKEA-style. Today, the place was packed, so I had to settle for a table closer to the front, instead of my favorite place further back in the room. The waiters all knew me, so I didn't have to ask for my coffee; it simply showed up at my table. Like the stranger who arrived at my table just after the coffee did. I hadn't even seen him walk up to me. One minute he wasn't there; the next he was sitting across the table from me.

He was very short, almost dwarflike, and dressed like a bum. With his petite size, he reminded me of Yoda, the great Jedi warrior from the Star Wars saga. He was also tan, which made me think he was one of the poorer class who worked outside. Chinese take great care to avoid the sun; white skin is the beauty standard, and indicates a person of wealth and stature. He was wizened, weird looking, and slumped over in his chair, causing his already shapeless clothes to bunch up all around him. The maître d' immediately came over, intent on ushering the man out. Instead, the "dwarf" ordered tea in perfect English, and the game had begun.

The voice did not match the creature. When he ordered cream and sugar to accompany his tea, his voice was commanding but not loud, and delivered in flawless English. I just sat there, not knowing what to say or do, or for that matter, think. When he spoke to me, I just stared at him.

"You're making an ass of yourself; worse, you are endangering not only your life but those of the people around you. I'll come by your apartment and explain how things will need to be done."

With that, he got up and walked out of the restaurant, leaving his perfectly ordered tea untouched. No one in the restaurant took notice, and even the maître d' seemed equally puzzled as the small man whizzed right past him and out into the street.

I stayed long enough to finish my coffee, and then it was time to go back to my office. My driver, Odd Job (my affectionate nickname for him), was waiting, and I asked if he had noticed anything peculiar. He shook his head and didn't seem in the least bit concerned. We returned to the school, and after a while the demands of my day replaced the image of the strange little man. But not for long.

Two nights later, I walked into my apartment, and there he was, sitting on my couch. Gone were the shabby clothes and downtrodden demeanor; instead, he was dressed impeccably, as if he had just stepped off Savile Row. His shirt was clearly custom-made and unusual for the city, given the dirty smog caused by diesel exhaust. It was pristinely white. The suit, pure Armani, and the shoes, Gucci. His gold cuff links were distinctively Dunhill, and I found myself staring at them. Today, as I write this, I have them in front of me on the desk. After Yoda died two years ago, his son brought them to me in Canada. I have never worn them, and only took them out as inspiration when I was writing about him. When this book is published, I will wear them in honor of the man who has kept Pink Pagoda flourishing.

The hunched, rumpled man was no longer. The man sitting in front of me sat tall and straight, and did not seem nearly as short as when I had first met him. This was the real Yoda, totally in control and focused.

With his perfectly manicured fingers, he placed a thick folder on the table between us. Even his fingers were unstained from tobacco smoke, not like most Chinese men, who are prolific smokers. For a moment, he just sat there and stared back at me as I looked in bemusement at the document in front of me.

How did he get in here? I wondered. Aside from Odd Job, who carefully scrutinizes everyone coming into the building, my strange visitor would have had to get past the lobby guard, and then the penthouse floor guard in order to get to my apartment. And how had he gotten in? My key worked as always, and there was no sign of a forced entry. He had simply, apparently, just "appeared" on my sofa.

"I know who you are, and I know the kind of work you are doing. It is good work, but you are in danger, along with those working for you. I do admire what you are doing, but you must do it differently. I will take care of that for you, and you will do exactly what I say."

What?! I didn't say the word out loud, but the look on my face was clear. He never mentioned Pink Pagoda, but it was also clear that my baby-saving program was what he was talking about.

"Read the document in front of you. It covers the eight months I have been watching you. When you read it, you will understand why I am here."

When he leaned slightly forward to indicate the folder, I noticed that he was wearing a gun. Very few Chinese, even police officers, have guns. His was secured in the middle of his back, and looked to be a Walther PPK, best known to the world as James Bond's signature gun.

At this point, most people who know me might wonder why I just didn't say, "Who the heck are you, anyway?" I didn't. Something in me knew that I should listen and hold myself in check. I wasn't afraid, just off balance. Clearly, I was no longer the one in control when it came to Pink Pagoda.

"Of this you can be certain: You have my assurance that you will be kept safe, along with your family and team. My people will take care of you, but you must obey me completely."

It felt like a scene out of a movie, one of those Mob movies in which the "patron" is indicating to the newly made man that as long as he obeys the man in charge, his life will be fine. I asked him to keep going, and he did.

"My experience in this area is that I know the intelligence community. I am in that community; I know that community and it knows me. There is respect for who I am, and that respect will extend to you."

I nodded to indicate that I understood, and he continued.

"Do you have any questions? Do I need to clarify anything?"

"No, I understand. You want to be in charge, and in return you protect me. I like being protected, and all I want is to keep the babies and my people safe."

He nodded in return.

"A foreigner like you is a rare thing, and you do honor to Dr. Bethune."

That was all he said. Our very brief, maybe thirty-minute meeting, was over. He got up and left as unobtrusively as when he had entered. He closed the door quietly behind him, leaving me to look at the document he had left behind. I took a quick look, and it was indeed "my life at a glance." Every detail of the past eight months was there, down to the most excruciating detail. I was stunned, but somehow not really surprised.

I decided to go downstairs and ask if anybody might know who this man was. I planned to have a translator ask Odd Job, who didn't speak English, if he had noticed my visitor. Down in the lobby, he was sitting with the guards at the desk, sipping tea and talking. When I walked over, I had one of the men who spoke a little English pose my question to my driver. Odd Job looked at me calmly as he answered through the translator.

"Not to worry, Dr. Garrow. Not to worry."

9

INTERVIEW WITH CRAIG AND KATHY

I really did try not to worry, about almost everything. Since childhood, my motto had been to move ahead and not look back over my shoulder. That biblical story about Lot and the pillar of salt that used to be his wife* made a lasting impression on me. I had also learned through all of my ventures and adventures to trust my feet, like a Sherpa climber. No matter how narrow the ledge or how long the drop, if I trusted my inner feet, I would be able to reach my destination.

While that visit from Yoda hadn't unnerved me, it had begun over the next few months to make me feel as though someone had thrown a few pebbles under those Sherpa feet. I found myself looking for some kind of touchstone, maybe a little of that cliché I so hate—a reality check of sorts.

My entire life I had been a man set on making money and lots of it. I had; I still did. Now I was on a new journey where I was still making lots of money, but I was also spending lots of it to save baby girls and change the lives of parents who would otherwise remain childless. So now, always having been a man who backs everything up with records and receipts, I came up with an idea. I didn't share it with anyone, because in a way I thought it almost seemed silly. It wasn't silly to me.

*Genesis 19

Craig and Kathy had been my first adoptive parents, and I wanted there to be some record of their experience, something to show people somewhere down the road how things had gone with that first adoption. I've read lots of interviews where the moderator is actually the subject of the interview, and some of those were actually very revealing, very honest. Maybe I could do one of those with Craig and Kathy. Then posterity, whoever, whatever, might have a record of how it all started. What the heck? It was worth a call to them.

I gave them a call, explained what I wanted to do, and not surprisingly, they said yes without hesitation. I didn't hear any surprise or stifled laughter in their voices, so I was beginning to think maybe this was a good idea after all. We agreed on a time, and I sent them the questions I wanted to ask so they'd have time to think about them. I set up the free conference call, and we were good to go.

"Hi, Craig; hi, Kathy. I really want to thank you two for doing this. It's a bit offbeat, but then, both of you know that my path is slightly skewed from most, eh?"

"Not a problem, Jim; we're glad to help the world know how profoundly you are changing people's lives, and a record of that is a good thing. Let's do this!"

And with that, our interview began.

JG: It's hard to believe that it's been nearly three years since I asked you that propitious question.

CRAIG: Oh, you mean, "So, do you want a baby now?"

JG: Yes, that one. I can still see your face, as if you must be thinking that I had a supply somewhere of babies for adoption. Well, for those who don't know anything about how we met or came to know each other, why don't you fill them in?

CRAIG: Well, it certainly wasn't from a business connection. I was an expat living in Chongqing; and like most of us Canadians, hockey games and good beer were a regular part of our entertainment. In fact, it's sort of odd that you and I didn't really get to know each other until I smashed you in the face during one of those games. You just don't smash into the goalie like that, and so I told you that I owed you a beer.

JG: Yeah, I remember, but it was a little while before we finally got together over a couple of Heinekens.

CRAIG: Usually, we guys talk about sports and what's going on in our jobs; but I remember that I felt really comfortable with you, and so I shared that my wife and I had not been able to have a child of our own, and that we were thinking about adopting. Since I was going to be in China for a while, my wife, who was a teacher back in the States, would leave it to me to check out the possibilities of adopting a Chinese baby girl. That's basically how it all started.

JG: Had you looked into traditional adoption agencies in China?

CRAIG: Oh, sure, but not only were they outrageously expensive; they were also very slow in being able to provide a baby.

JG: Now, other people might wonder how you happened to ask a Canadian hockey buddy whose obvious business was running Chinese schools about adopting a baby.

CRAIG: It really wasn't so much that I asked you, specifically; it's more that you asked me point-blank, "Hey, do you want a baby girl?"

JG: Right, right. But I remember that you didn't seem to skip a beat in saying yes.

CRAIG: Well, it's fair to say that your reputation preceded you; and I just knew—no, trusted—that your word was dependable. Plus, everyone seemed to know that you had major guanxi with the Chinese, and with the expats.

JG: But I told you up front that you would be adopting a baby under very unusual circumstances. Right?

CRAIG: Oh, yeah, you were very clear that what we would be doing was absolutely illegal, and that all the paperwork would be forged.

JG: And that didn't bother you, becoming a sort of criminal, I mean?

CRAIG: I didn't really think of it in those exact terms. Everyone on the Canadian hockey team in particular knew that you were scrupulously honest, and that you wouldn't do anything wacky or stupid. I think a lot of things that are done for the sake of humanity are probably illegal in one way or another. As long as I could depend on you to do what you said you would, I wasn't concerned.

JG: What about you, Kathy? What did you think when Craig called you and asked if you wanted to adopt a baby girl—*now*?

KATHY: I don't think it took me even a minute to say yes. First of all, I trust Craig, and if he trusted you, I wasn't concerned. He was up front with me about the adoption being technically illegal; I preferred to focus on "technically." Those of us in this country remember the story of the Underground Railroad back in America's slave days, when it was illegal to help any slave trying to escape to the North. People did it anyway. It was a matter of the greatest good over the lesser wrong.

JG: Well, in that respect I'd have to say that I have a bit of an American sensibility.

KATHY: In fact, I remember that I told Craig to do the adoption right away. I didn't hesitate at all, and, Jim, it was the best decision of our lives. You're responsible for giving us our beautiful daughter. I wish that you were able to see her, be around her. That would show you just how massively important your work is.

JG: Thanks, Kathy; I acknowledge that every single day, and I'm truly grateful to God that I'm able to continue saving those little lives. But back to the actual adoption process for a moment, you must have had some concerns and fears. What was your greatest concern or fear?

CRAIG: For me, it was worrying about getting our new baby back into the United States without any problems, and wanting to be sure that she would be an American citizen, like with any other "legal" adoption from another country. But that fear didn't last very long. All of the paperwork was proper, and you made sure that we had affiliation with an organization and were part of a specific, numbered group. My one fear was natural, but it turned out to be needless.

JG: Kathy, what about you? Did you have any fear?

KATHY: At first, a little, just like Craig, wondering if we'd have any trouble when we got back to the United States. But clearly, and I saw that for myself in China, everybody seemed to know who you were. Even walking down the street, Chinese people, even monks, just looked at you, and tried not to crowd you. I don't know exactly what that was all about, but you definitely had presence and respect. You made me feel safe, and confident about adopting our little girl.

JG: What about when the two of you got back safely into the United States? Did you ever worry that someone might show up at your door and confront you about the adoption?

CRAIG: Never. Not once. Kathy and I knew that you'd involved three different organizations to sort of watch over us, and we always felt protected.

KATHY: And what I noticed was that you had planned in advance for any kind of detail, any contingency that might go wrong, and you were totally prepared. There were real agencies involved as well. It was clear to me that you had covered all your bases.

JG: Let's go back to that moment when you saw your baby for the first time. Tell me about that.

CRAIG: I'll let Kathy go first.

KATHY: Wow, that was something else . . . Sorry. I still get choked up when I remember. Love at first sight; that's exactly what it was. Excitement. Tears. It was more emotional than I could have imagined.

CRAIG: I think for me it was more like beautiful disbelief. It was just amazing. And looking at Kathy holding our baby. Even I get choked up remembering. What about you, Jim? I mean, this was the first baby you had saved, and here you were, watching her new parents welcoming her to her new life.

JG: Now who's choked up? There was a certain amount of disbelief for me, too, that I'd actually done this. Maybe even a little surreal.

KATHY: Oh, wait; and I also remember saying over and over again, "I can't believe it; I just can't believe it." And then I kept saying, "Thank you, Jim" over and over again, too. And all those tears.

CRAIG: But there was that funny comment you made. Remember?

KATHY: Oh, you mean, "I guess we'll have to sell the Camaro."

CRAIG: Right, our sweet little Camaro.

JG: Well, I guess that was a bit of a disappointment; I know you talked about that car during our beer chats. Was there any other surprise or even disappointment connected to the adoption? Anything you'd change?

KATHY: Oh, no, no real surprises and definitely no disappointments; but a big change, yes. I've always been a churchgoing woman, and when I came home with a baby, my entire universe changed. My church friends had always been very supportive of my wanting children, and now I had my sweet, baby girl. For the first time I felt like I really belonged, you know, with all those women and their children. People were just so loving and helpful. I don't think I could have predicted that.

JG: Craig, what about you?

CRAIG: Like Kathy, no disappointments or anything like that. Just one huge change: sleep. Or I should say, lack of sleep. Our little girl didn't settle in for quite a while. Kathy, being a teacher, thought it was probably that the baby was unaccustomed to all the different smells, sights, and sounds, all very different from what she experienced in China. Sound especially. The tonality of the Chinese voice is very different from the way Americans talk. It must have been almost scary for the baby.

KATHY: Absolutely. From the time a baby is in her mother's stomach, what that baby hears sounds almost like singing. The English language is nothing less than jarring by contrast. Eventually, our little baby settled in; but, yes, we did have a lot of sleepless nights.

JG: Another question. I know that you both wanted to adopt more than one baby. Aside from all those sleepless nights, why didn't you?

CRAIG: Yes, we would have liked to adopt other babies; but Kathy and I both agreed that it might jeopardize the little girl we already had. It just wasn't worth taking that chance, and we simply poured all of our love into the child we do have.

JG: You know, someone might wonder why you never use the name of your child.

CRAIG: I guess you could say that your organization trained us well. You just never know . . .

JG: Thanks. That's my job, along with making sure the money continues to flow.

KATHY: Now, that reminds me of the biggest surprise we encountered. No cost. I mean, not even our own expenses. And then you sent over that lovely Chinese girl to help our baby—and us—with the transition. And then she would send back pictures and little stories to Xinyi, so that everyone would know how happy and healthy the baby was. Your generosity was completely unexpected, and we will always be more grateful than we can ever express.

CRAIG: I have a question; I never really asked you before, but here goes. Do you extend that kind of generosity to all your adoptive parents?

JG: Yes and no. To the question of cost, there is never a cost to the new parents, ever; and, yes, we do help out if financial difficulties arise after the baby is home with her new parents. Sending you the girl to help out was something extra; we did that because this was our first adoption, and the baby was Xinyi's niece.

KATHY: People must love you for such extraordinary generosity.

JG: I'll quote Yoda on that one. "You will either be doomed or saved by the fact of your generosity." So far, I'm on the "saved" end of the pendulum swing. But I'm always conscious of those who might attack me.

CRAIG: You've got at least forty thousand believers, along with their parents. To use a word you're so close to, you've got universal *guanxi*. I don't think God's plan for you has the word "doom" in it.

JG: Thanks, Craig. I like to believe that's true.

KATHY: Well, Jim, this really has been lovely, but our little baby is now an adventurous toddler, and we need to go. We'll never be able to thank you enough, and I'm sure you hear that from other adoptive parents all the time. Anyway, God bless you and the work you do. You're always in our prayers.

CRAIG: Amen to that. Just think, it took a smack to the side of your head to release the angel in your heart. I remember your telling me that even though your mother was Jewish, you were raised as a Christian. Since this is all about mothers and babies, I'll use two of my favorite Jewish terms. You're a mensch, and there aren't enough *nachas* [blessings] in the world to honor what you do. Take care, Jim.

JG: Well, I think I'm going to take a little walk down into the city, away from the hotel. The Chongqing crud isn't so bad today, and I'll be sure to have my taxi card with me so that I don't have to be rescued by schoolchildren. I really appreciate your taking the time to talk with me. Everyone needs a sounding board now and then, and I wanted to reconnect with the two people whose adoption showed me what was possible. God bless you both.

After we hung up, I did go for a walk down toward the dirt-packed streets, wondering as I walked if there was a baby in danger behind one of the doors I passed. Not to worry. If there was, someone would tell me.
Later.

10

CHINESE PUZZLE

"Later" also brought with it a remembrance of what Yoda had said during that meeting in my apartment. Two Canadians, one linked destiny. Me and Dr. Bethune.

Yoda's reference to Dr. Bethune was not the first time I had heard that comparison. Since my first trip to China, people had told me outright that they believed I was the reincarnation of the revered doctor who revolutionized medical procedures during the Second Sino-Japanese War. For Americans who might not recognize his name, the term *MASH* is certainly a famous acronym, and it was Dr. Bethune, a Canadian by birth, who developed the mobile medical units that were precursors of the MASH (mobile army surgical hospital) units instituted in 1945, after his death. Bethune's mobile units, along with the MASH units that followed, were responsible for saving so many lives during the wars of his century, worldwide. The Bethune Institute was and is a paean to his legacy, which in some nearly inexplicable way, I have inherited. Using his name wasn't so much a strategic move on my part as it was a dynamic, spiritual one. Throughout China, there are numerous other "Bethune" epithets; in one case, a urology institute in Beijing actually called me to get permission before using his name for their organization. I might have been surprised or even shocked that anyone would think that I had some proprietary control over his name, except that I had come to accept there was at the very least a strong connection between the two of us.

I am a Christian, and do not believe in reincarnation. Not exactly. What I know for certain is that there is some undefined, spiritual connection between the good doctor and me. I prefer to think that I operate in the style of Dr. Bethune, working in the guise of a man who is an internationalist and who loves the Chinese people enough to spend my own resources on their behalf—without restriction or any consideration for a particular ethnic group. It is similar to my being called "President Jim" at that inaugural banquet in my honor during my first trip to China. "President"? I would never perceive myself as a revered leader, but I came to accept—even if I didn't fully understand—that I was somehow "known" in China, even though I was a foreigner whose first trip was ostensibly to start up a network of schools.

When I later found myself as the originating force behind Pink Pagoda, my reputation expanded to include another iconic name: Robin Hood.

Most people would not put the names Bethune and Robin Hood in the same sentence, unless of course they're talking about Jim Garrow. Let me be clear. I may indeed be somehow following in Dr. Bethune's footsteps, but I am not Robin Hood, rescuing babies from one family to give to another. For one thing, Robin is presumed to have taken at least a small share of the spoils for his hard-earned labor, and he was not especially concerned for the safety of his merry band of men. I have never, from baby 1 to baby 40,000 and counting, solicited or been paid even the smallest amount of financial compensation. I pay the expenses from the earnings derived from my schools in China, and I put in my own personal money whenever the situation demands it. Since the inception of my program, I have conservatively spent millions of dollars to ensure that no baby goes unsaved. Back home in Guelph, Ontario, I drive a twelve-year-old car, and I do not live extravagantly by any definition. Those who know me at my home can certainly attest to that.

Another piece of the puzzle that connects my life to others is the legacy of Mao Tse-tung, whose one-child policy was the direct stimulus to the founding of Pink Pagoda. Mao's original view was that one could dominate one's enemies by controlling the ethnic group from which they came. For Mao, that group was the Han. In his struggle for Communist elitism, he began the tragic war against baby girls. In my determined effort to save that first baby girl, I began to wage war against him and the concept of elitism by any political name or group.

But then a truly strange thought made its way into my contemplative consciousness. It almost came to me like the parts of a syllogism:

Dr. Bethune, a Canadian, comes to China, and his good work is recognized and honored by the most powerful Chinese leader of that time, Mao Tse-tung.

Mao Tse-tung, in his idealistic but misguided and myopic view of how to make China a better country, imposes a one-child mandate aimed at the Han, who are his political enemies and who he believes are threatening the future of his country.

Dr. Garrow, a Canadian, comes to China to make Chinese schools more productive and finds himself becoming an idealistic but misguided and myopic crusader (an ass, in Yoda's words) whose efforts to save babies are creating danger that may impact hundreds if not thousands of people.

Conclusion of syllogism: Dr. James Garrow has something in common with Mao Tse-tung. Without falling prey to a logical "undistributed middle," it would appear that Mao's destiny and mine were linked.

I stop contemplating for a moment. This wasn't a light bulb moment; it was a spotlight, and I was standing in the middle of it. What to think?

I came back, mentally, to a place of *ching an*, "clear space." The logical, connective tissue here is a term I could never have understood if I weren't living and working in China: *guanxi*.

The actual meaning of the Mandarin word is fairly simple. It means "relationships," but as most terms with a five-thousand-year history of development, it has actually evolved into a very complex and intricate dance between simple and complex. Let's look at a more modern-day example.

If you and I were friends in China, we would say that we shared guanxi; but if I had gone to Beijing University and you had gone to Nanjing University, I would be considered to have more guanxi than you. At this level, guanxi is equivalent to status.

If, through some set of circumstances, I then developed a relationship with a high-ranking government official, I would be considered to have great guanxi, which now includes influence.

Guanxi can also extend to living in the right building, driving the right car, wearing the right clothes, going to the right club, having the right flair, and having the right friends.

All of this comes down to one absolute reality. Guanxi trumps law.

If I get stopped by a policeman in China for some traffic violation, that officer has to determine if my guanxi exceeds his. If it does, then he has to consider whether the ticket—which is arguably part of his duty and the law—might cost him his job because of the offending driver's guanxi. The officer has to be able to determine in that moment if the risk of issuing a ticket may, in fact, come back to bite him. He also knows that to lie about one's guanxi will bring swift retribution, so his choice in my case would be to refrain from citing me. I, in turn, would reciprocate by offering him a coupon for a good restaurant, his knowing that I will pay for that meal. Now the officer has new guanxi with me, a powerful person, and the guanxi escalates for both of us because now the restaurant owner who recognizes my name on the coupon has a new respect for the officer, and I now have new guanxi with the restaurant owner. A lot of "now this, and then that," and that is exactly how guanxi works.

The cardinal understanding of guanxi is that at the highest levels it is not necessary to use guanxi at all. There is no need to ask or demand; it is understood that at some future point in time, reciprocity will be given, usually at a higher level than the original guanxi offer. My red-and-gold passport document is a testament to how high up my guanxi goes. Moving money in China is a heavily proscribed activity with severe limits. I have none.

This significant exchanging of favors must also be done regularly and voluntarily. More globally, it is perceived as a kind of force that makes the world go round. If a Chinese person brings in someone who can resolve a problem, that person is said to have "good guanxi." In my own experience, and even though after doing business in China for more than five years, I had only managed to learn a few words of Mandarin, my ability to communicate and "resolve things" established me as a man of powerful guanxi. It was my original connection with those first Chinese students back at Shaw College that had initiated my unqualified acceptance by everyone from Chinese officials to those who serve as drivers and employees, all the way to the bong-bong men who scavenge from the streets of the city. Beggars or kings, I felt connections with people from all walks of life. Guanxi is so much more than just networking.

The final part of the puzzle, and the one that at first made me rather uncomfortable, is that of the "mystic tradition." Most people think of a mystic as a highly enlightened person who leads a rather austere life, and who may or may not have divinely sourced visions.

I am not that kind of mystic.

By classical definition, a mystic is one who is determined to lead a useful life in the service of others, and to expect no earthly reward for doing so.

I'm that kind of mystic, and Pink Pagoda is my temple of choice.

11

HIDING IN PLAIN SIGHT

On a mystic path, with guanxi as my parable, I was keenly aware that every action I produced, every relationship I engaged in, would have a ripple effect beyond whatever I could perceive in the present moment. What at first had seemed to be more of a Chinese puzzle was becoming more and more of a cohesive matrix.

With all those puzzle pieces in place, I had become an easily recognized figure throughout China. Now Yoda wanted me to "hide in plain sight."

Excuse me?

Since Yoda had taken over, my participation in Pink Pagoda had been strictly behind-the-scenes. I provided the money, and he and his "cells" took care of everything else. A smart plan, this lifted my schools out of the adoption process and provided the highest possible level of security for everyone involved. I respected and accepted that I was, to any public scrutiny, out of the picture. It was a surprise, therefore, when I got a call from Yoda asking—no, insisting—that we meet.

I was just about to head out for dinner at the Crowne Plaza when my cell phone rang. Because no identifying number showed up, I knew I should take the call. Yoda didn't believe in voicemail, and I was sure it must be him.

"Hello?"

The question in my voice just needed to be sure.

"Where are you?"

Yoda's question was unnecessary. He already knew where I was.

Even though his voice sounded a little like the cartoon character Lisa Simpson, his voice was unmistakable.

"You know where I am; why do you ask?" I smiled as I responded.

Yoda had on many previous occasions told me that he always knew where I was, but that it just seemed polite to ask. Not only did he know which city I was in at any given time; he could also list all the places I'd been that particular day. At first, knowing that I was so easily tracked had me a bit on edge. After a while, and seeing all the ways that Yoda had, as he would say, "saved our bacon" (his favorite Western food), I became comfortable with being watched over instead of being watched.

"V Bar?" Yoda asked.

"Sure. Tell me when."

We arranged to meet an hour later. Since the restaurant was part of the hotel's resort-style complex, I would have enough time to grab a quick bite and then meet up with him. Rather than have Odd Job drive me, I decided to walk. My recent experience at the temple outside Shanghai had left me feeling drained and devastated beyond any definition of that word. Not now; I couldn't think about that now. I had to stay in the present and get to the meeting with Yoda.

Instead of going through the lobby, I chose instead to use one of the side entrances away from the main street, Nanjing Road East. I walked past the outdoor pool area, done up with a sand beach, grass huts, and palm trees. The tropics seemed almost natural in their Oriental setting. I stopped for a moment, partly to enjoy the peacefulness of the scenery, but also to watch several families with young children enjoying the evening warmth, not wanting to surrender to the chill of the night. Thinking of that chill began to remind me of death, and I had to move on. I took a deep breath, my nostrils filled with the smell of chlorine and the smoky scent of newly lit tiki torches.

After dinner, I took a back table at the V Bar. Even though it was early, the place was already alive with Western businessmen, together with a few of their Chinese colleagues and hosts. I tried to tune out all the buzz by burying myself in the book I had brought along, Peter Hessler's *River Town: Two Years on the Yangtze*—soon to become *"James Garrow: Five*

Days on the Yangtze."

Just as I had begun reading, Yoda appeared suddenly and plucked the book out of my hands. He dangled the book in front of him, looking as if he had just caught a prize trout. In waving the book about, he snapped the spine. Then, holding the book up toward the lights, he started to read, but not before retrieving his reading glasses, with a scowl.

"Vanity, thy name is man." Yoda peered out over the top of his glasses, looking almost professorial. "When you are my age, you will understand. Maybe, with your prescience you won't have to wait so long."

Before I could ask him to explain that cryptic comment, he sat down. He did not offer to shake my hand, and I knew better than to offer mine. I did order him his favorite beer, Heineken, and watched him twist off the bottle cap with his short, sausage-like fingers. He took a sip, and I couldn't help but notice that his right pinkie finger was bent. I had asked him once before how that had happened, and his icy stare told me never to ask the question again. He did not seem to appreciate my humor in calling his digit "the Defector," the only finger not conforming to the rest of the hand.

After exchanging a few pleasantries, he sat quietly and scanned the ceiling.

"Is everything okay?" I knew better than to ever address him by name.

"Like you, I'm tired. I've been very busy, as you already know."

I nodded. We both knew that his responsibilities in Pink Pagoda were much more difficult than mine. I never asked him about his job. I referred to what he did for me as "moonlighting." It was a small joke between us. The Chinese use the moon to delineate dates, while they use the sun to identify months. Confusing to a Westerner, but a significant part of the overlap between our two worlds.

This meeting also constituted an overlap between his role and mine in Pink Pagoda. The daily operations of the program he had established was to depend on communications with and from the "Coffee Drinkers" and the "Decision Makers." The Coffee Drinkers kept their eyes peeled and ears to the ground for information about babies needing to be rescued. They would then pass along that information along to the Decision Makers, who would then analyze the data and decide whether or not to approach Yoda about a rescue attempt. Most of the Coffee Drinkers were women because of their ability to "hear" things that men might not. Women were a crucial part of the process at all levels. Yoda appreciated that, but he also saw no problem in bringing in a male when trying to "close the deal" with a woman facing the loss of her child. I disagreed, but Yoda's choices always prevailed. Keep in mind, too, that prior to Yoda's operation, we only rescued babies when someone approached us. Yoda's program was all about outreach, with safety nets built in. We paid for all of their living expenses, along with their yearly salary. There are those who might say that we were "paying them off." Absolutely not. By taking excellent care of our people, we ensured the most professional and loyal staff. If one of our Coffee Drinkers was exposed and then subject to fines or imprisonment, we (meaning, I) would take care of their fines and compensate them for any lost time or inconvenience. That rarely happened, thanks to Yoda's self-contained "cells," which provided strong separation among its members. This is where China's immense size proved advantageous.

The Chinese government agencies are also layered in this way. Most people in the West may perceive China as having a central government under the direct control of Hu Jintao, when, in actual fact, government rule is scattered throughout provinces all over the country. The People's Republic of China is far removed from the lives of everyday people, who look far more to their local governances for what they need.

This particular evening, Yoda was about to present me with a substantial exception to his rule about my staying "invisible" and only becoming directly involved in any of the actions when "absolutely necessary."

"How would you like to go on a cruise down the Yangtze River?" He tapped his Defector on the table as he posed the question. Except that it really wasn't a question at all.

I asked the most obvious question in return.

"From where to where? And when?"

"In two days, leaving from here. You arrive in Shanghai five days later, back in Chongqing the day after that. Six days total."

"So, you're shanghaiing me to Shanghai?"

I simply couldn't resist. Nor could he resist ordering another beer.

"Yes," he replied. "Have you been before?"

"Both," I mumbled. "Yes to both."

Now it was his turn to look puzzled, and mine to look concerned.

12

ROLLING DOWN
THE RIVER

Two days later, I boarded the Viking Cruise Line's river "luxury" cruiser, the *Victoria*. With me were two Chinese women from Chongqing who gave me their names as Yuk and Jun. I knew, of course, that those were aliases, and smiled at the meaning of the words—Yuk means "moon," and Jun means "truth." I had no doubt that Yoda had chosen those names with a twist of ironic humor in mind. Jun, a petite girl with a broad smile, was carrying the baby girl we were transporting to Shanghai, where the infant would be passed on to our people there. Later, she would travel to her new home in Canada. Min, the baby's mother, was also with us, spending most of her time standing at the rail. The water below was the color of café au lait, not clear and green, as one might expect. Min herself was not exactly what I expected. With her squat stature and round face, she reminded me of a pigeon, wearing her dingy gray Mao jacket. Her hair was cut short and shagged its way to her collar, where it did its best to produce a flip. All I knew about her was she came from a relatively small town in the Henan province, an area best known for its agriculture, especially sesame, wheat, and rice. In a way, she reminded me a bit of a country yokel, and our little group certainly seemed to stick out on this rather elegant cruise. As we all "hid in plain sight," it was assumed that I would appear to be either an expat or an American businessman; I would have preferred *Jianada* to *Megwa*. Yuk and Jun would be my "wife's" relatives. Robin and his merry band of women . . .

There was the issue of Min's clothes. In her dingy clothes, she didn't look like someone who could afford a cruise that easily cost two thousand bucks. Hiding in plain sight couldn't exactly be that plain.

Yuk and Jun, who became to me "Truth-Moon," offered to take her into town and buy her more suitable clothes. They returned with a much more stylish version of Min. There wasn't anything to be done about her pigeon quality. One would probably never have guessed that she was a person of influence in her own town, and that Yoda placed enough importance on her future cooperation to set up this particular excursion.

Min was a member of the Communist Party and powerful enough to already have two children. A third child, this baby, was out of the question, thus her presence during this trip. I had briefly held the child when the girls went on their shopping expedition, and it struck me just how close this baby had come to being set aside if we had not intervened. So close.

By showing Min how carefully we operated, Yoda hoped to extend our adoption reach into Henan, which is the second most populous province in China. In order to continue saving babies, we had to think of our enterprise as a business, and allies were essential to our operation. This adoption was sensational in the true sense of the word. Although this particular mission could have been construed as high-risk, it would clearly show that we could handle ourselves out in the open. It was a daring move on Yoda's part, but I never doubted that he had everything under control. Yoda also knew that Min had a complicated sense of loyalty to her party and to local officials, based upon her own family background. We had a way "in," and we had to, in fact, put on a good show.

Min firmly believed that a child could thrive when raised by other than the birth parents, although Yoda and I did not discuss such issues with her. Nor was she worried about reprisals from within the Party. She was highly placed within its organization, and guanxi would prevent others from revealing anything about her actions. Guanxi was also working on our behalf. Unlike Xinyi, Min did not immediately trust us. Like so many desperate mothers in China, she had been approached by those bottom-feeders who seek out babies for human trafficking and the sex trades. Yoda and I had to be especially careful in our dealings with her. A pleasure cruise this was not.

After we first disembarked, I retreated to my room. The *Victoria* was touted as a luxury cruiser, and at more than three hundred feet in length, it cut a striking figure in the water. China was still nurturing its travel profile, and this boat was obviously in its makeover stage. Both we and the ship were attempting to be something more than what we really were.

On board, the ship did offer standard luxury liner fare: nightly entertainments, gaming, and a profusion of never-ending buffets which ran the gamut from moo shu to macaroni and cheese. This blending of Chinese and Westernized Chinese dishes was one of the ship's biggest attractions. Not so attractive was sharing meals with a woman, Min, whose table manners were more akin to a feral dog's. I don't mean that to sound cruel; it was just that she had no experience with knives, forks, and spoons. Think Iowa corn farmer with chopsticks, trying to eat noodle soup. She also ate her food *mit gusto*, which to an observer more closely resembled gustatory diving.

Food aside, there were also some stops along our itinerary that looked intriguing to me. One was the hill Shibaozhai, renowned for its eighteenth-century architectural marvel—a red wood pagoda clinging to the side of the cliff, seven hundred feet above the Yangtze. While the wrong color to symbolize our own pagoda, it was an impressive sight. To reach the top, we had to climb twelve stories of steps carved out of the side of the rocky cliff, and for this part of our trip, Min, with her swift sprints, was the full-out winner. We, on the other hand, arrived with barely enough breath to express our wonder at the sight before us. Up here, the belching, noxious plumes of smoke rising from the industrial cities and town below could be viewed as hope for a more prosperous China. Min was determined to be part of that development and growth.

Min wasn't the only person of interest in Yoda's sights; he had also arranged for me to meet with two other women who could be very helpful to us. Meeting people face-to-face is the ultimate networking scenario, and I was the designated netter. Again, Yoda's offer of a pleasure cruise was a full-service gambit for me.

The real pleasure of this cruise was in saving a child's life and transporting her to a new home. It was also very sad to watch Min as the miles floated by, her knowing that with each mile the time with her daughter was ebbing away. While I listened to the guide talking about occult artifacts, entombed coffins, and the ancient Ba people who gave their name to this region, I also observed Min responding to the howls of monkeys nearby. She held her daughter up in the air, repeating "monkey" over and over again. She would never know if her child remembered.

The night before we were about to disembark in Shanghai, I stood out on the deck, sharing my solitude with a shaft of moonlight that seemed to illuminate my thoughts as well. I thought of my mother, who was in ill health. It was she and her devout Christian beliefs that had led—no, pushed—me into the work I was doing now. Had she not been so passionate about doing good in the world, this baby in our care would be doomed, because I would have been somewhere else.

There was also the matter of coincidences. I needed to start work at Shaw College in order for that first group of Chinese students to invite me to China and launch me into starting schools, leading me to hire Xinyi . . . and the rest is already written.

Floating past those cliffs, their stony shoulders bore witness to the beauty of the universe, contrasted with the frequent ugliness of its dwellers. Here I was, traveling with a woman who was willing to consider the sacrifice of her own daughter in order to satisfy a cruel, human edict. The Chinese were about to alter the course of the Yangtze for their own purposes; Min was altering the course of her life to save one.

Arriving in Shanghai, I was relieved but not surprised to find the baby's documents waiting for us. Min was now assured that all of our intentions and actions were true. A few hours later, we were all standing at the airport, each of us about to head off in a different direction. Jun, still holding the child, offered her to Min for one last embrace. Min shuddered more than cringed, and pulled back, shaking her head. My last image of her was as she hurried into one of those stores that sells neck cushions and travel apparatus. She looked lost among all those cushions, as if wondering how anything so small could offer her comfort.

My comfort was in walking away empty-handed.

13

THE GREAT
WAILING WALL

Walking away empty-handed may have soothed my soul, but my mind was still sadly unquiet. On the one hand, I dearly loved the Chinese people. When I was in China, I felt as if I were at home, as though I belonged there. I did belong there, but my Christian faith was coming up hard against the Buddhist belief in reincarnation that was being used as an explanation, a justification, for being able to set aside an unwanted daughter.

Yoda, with his astute insight into the minds of people, including mine, saw that he had to do something.

Although Yoda had been raised as a Buddhist, he wasn't religious and followed his own sense of spiritual direction. He did believe that there were spiritual forces working in and around us, and that we had to be mindful and in touch with those. Because of those beliefs, he wanted me to visit a very special Buddhist temple.

"I have arranged for you to visit a place which I think you must see. Two of my associates will accompany you. I think that seeing this temple will be good for you."

I didn't ask for further explanation; it was like his invitation to go down the Yangtze on a pleasure cruise. Only one word from me.

"Sure."

The next day his two associates arrived, and "spirited" me away on our little journey.

"Dr. Garrow, we are going to show you something which may shock you, but it will give you an understanding of what we Chinese think and where we come from."

Their words were cryptic, but I presumed I would understand more when we arrived at our destination.

We headed for Yunnan province, about two hours from the city of Kunming. When we reached the temple, my two escorts handed me off to a small group of priests who gestured to me that I should follow them. None of them spoke any English, so nothing was said for the duration of my tour.

When we arrived at the parking lot, we parked, then walked across a bridge that led us to a wide set of marble stairs that would start our journey up the steep hillside. The steps were easily sixty feet wide and were flanked by carefully tended garden spaces with manicured trees and ornamental shrubs. Most people when they think of Oriental gardens think of Japanese gardens, but the Chinese are masters of horticulture and the concept of feng shui. I do have to add that while many Westerners invoke the concept of feng shui both in their homes and gardens, I am convinced that the classic definition of the term is lost on them.

After the first set of stairs and a level place above them, again with more gardens, we climbed another set, and then another as we zigzagged our way up the hill. When we finally reached the temple, we had climbed only two hundred feet in elevation, but the linear distance was easily a few hundred yards. I was breathless; not so the monks who had greeted me at the beginning of our journey. In fact, I felt as if I were being hustled, literally, as if we had some kind of time constraint for our trip. During my time in China, I have visited at least twenty-five different buddhas all over China, and all of those had one thing in common. No one rushed; everyone moved slowly, reflectively. I couldn't have reflected if I tried. This felt more like one of those European tours I have reluctantly agreed to take, where the landscape and buildings of interest are like a photograph taken at the wrong speed. What I did see as I climbed was indeed beautiful, but I would like to have had more time to stop and just say, "Ahhh."

Finally we were at the temple's entrance, and we walked in to see a sitting buddha that had to have been at least sixty feet tall. Although bronze in composition, its patina had taken on that kind of coppery green that comes from age and oxidation. It was indeed impressive, but again I was not being given more than a moment or two before we walked to the right of the buddha and behind it to a door in the back wall. At that point, I was handed over to four new monks, who continued the pace set by the first four.

More stairs, but this time leading down toward a small valley. These stairs were made of wood, and not nearly so wide as their marble counterparts. More stairs to the right, then to the left; then we reached a steep, rough terrain, which we proceeded to climb. At the top, I was looking across a valley about five hundred yards wide. It wasn't a deep valley, and I could see across to a meandering wall that looked something like a miniature version of the Great Wall.

I felt sure that this part of the temple grounds was not part of the usual tour, and I could not imagine why I was being brought here.

At this point, the monks motioned me to move ahead on my own, so I walked toward the wall. From a distance, I thought I was looking at bundles of wood stacked neatly up to the point of a narrow pagoda-style roof, presumably to keep the wood safe from rain. Overall, I took the wall to be about one hundred feet long and about five feet high. As I got closer still, it looked as though the bundles had been wrapped in very elaborately embroidered brocade, mostly red backgrounds with brightly colored embellishments. The bundles at the top were still vividly colored, but as my eyes moved toward the bottom of the wall, the bundles were more faded and tattered.

I was now directly in front of the wall, and close enough to touch the packages if I wanted to. I didn't; I couldn't.

My arms hung limply at my sides, and it felt as if all the air in my lungs had been sucked out of me. I don't remember for certain if I said anything. If I did, it would have been, "Oh, my God."

This is what Yoda had wanted me to see. This is what his associates had said would somehow shock me into a better understanding of the Chinese people. This is what the silence of the priests was speaking to me.

I was looking at a wall made up of dead babies, beautifully and lovingly wrapped in ceremonial fabrics. Given how many bundles there were, I had to be looking at hundreds and hundreds of bodies. My senses were frozen. Even my sense of smell, morbidly alert for any odor, detected nothing. This entire wall was frozen in time. And the wall was not yet fully formed. There would be more bundles, and new layers of grief. Grief for each new pair of parents who would bring their baby to the monks to be set aside, grief for the priests who would carry out the devastating task, and the grief of the universe for having lost one of its children.

After a few minutes, the blood began to return to my limbs, and I turned slowly and awkwardly toward the waiting group of priests. Nothing was said, no gestures offered except to follow them back down the steep hillside. Down at the bottom, the two men who had brought me here said nothing as they took me back to the car. I got in, and fell more than sat down on the seat.

"How in heaven's name do you justify this?"

My voice was somewhere between a croak and a rant. We did have a brief conversation about Buddhism and reincarnation, but I was too emotionally spent to appreciate the finer points of their discourse. I felt far less respect for Buddhists than I previously had, and all I could think about was getting a stiff drink. That, and find a game of hockey to jump into.

Striking images were crowding my head—the sight of my newborn son so close to death, the sight of Xinyi sobbing in my office, the sight of Min lost among neck cushions, trying to escape her anguish, and now the sight of a wall whose bricks had been, were, human.

There had to be other walls; I had seen only one. And there would be more walls to come. I felt like Hadrian building a wall against his enemies, only I was on a mission to prevent walls from being constructed. Back home, I grabbed that stiff drink and then headed out in search of a hockey game. I was in luck, and the Zambonis would have their work cut out for them after my performance. I slammed; I pushed; I hit. My rage was in every move I made.

That night, one of my favorite Pink Floyd songs became my new, personal anthem.

"Just another brick in the wall . . . Teacher, leave those kids alone."

It wasn't the teachers I had to worry about.

14

CRISIS OF FAITH
RESOLVED

Over the next couple of days, I came to understand why Yoda had insisted that I visit that temple. It wasn't that he didn't respect my Christian beliefs; it was that he felt my own beliefs had to be put in the context of his Chinese culture. I also have to admit that as the number of adoptions we were handling increased, the immensity of the problem had begun to wear on me. There were also those difficult adoptions where negotiations or delivery had proved problematic, and of course there was also my pleasure cruise experience on the Yangtze. Spending five days with a mother giving up her daughter in painful increments had been excruciating for me, and that image of her holding up her baby for the last time was only compounded by the sight of her lost among those neck cushions at the airport.

On the one hand, I knew that I was doing the right thing for these otherwise doomed babies. On the other hand, I was operating as a criminal in the eyes of the Chinese government, and our operations were always fraught with the possibility of danger and failure, regardless of how well prepared we believed ourselves to be. Yes, Yoda was an amazing architect for the Pink Pagoda, but even with his expertise we both knew that on any given day something could go horribly wrong. We did encounter a handful of such crises, and we learned from everything that happened. I can't say more about these, at risk of revealing too much about our day-to-day operations. Suffice it to say that in all these instances, both Yoda and I were devastated. Devastation, interpreted in the right, spiritual way, can actually create stronger determination. That is exactly what happened to us.

The other crisis of faith I had been dealing with was about Yoda himself. When he had originally come to me and proclaimed that he would be taking over our operation, I was at first very relieved. My number one concern was and still is that we rescue as many babies as we possibly can. What I hadn't expected was what it would be like to trade control and stewardship for protection. I had gone from being the guy in charge, a role I have always performed at maximum confidence and efficiency, to the hands-off "money guy." It wasn't so much a matter of ego as it was a sense of loss at having been replaced within my own organization. At some level, I felt almost like a failure for not having been able to manage the program I was so passionately connected to. I knew and accepted that Yoda was right, and that his way was the only way to keep Pink Pagoda alive. I had been humbled in God's eyes, and I was grateful for all He had given me, especially Yoda. I was and will forever be in awe of what we have all achieved, and for the remarkable connection with Yoda, and now his son. I remember that line from Mel Brooks's iconic film *History of the World, Part I*, in which the French king proclaims in an aside to the audience, "It's good to be the king." It's also good to be in the company of one.

When Yoda took over, we had roughly forty employees in 22 provinces; that number quickly grew to 142. At the beginning of Yoda's command and at his request, all of us came together for a celebratory dinner at Windows on the World, in a city offering access into Hong Kong. We had asked everyone to come in for three days. One of those days was all about doing touristy stuff, the second was spent with me, and the third involved Yoda. As it turned out, a disembodied Yoda. Our meeting was in a conference room where the speakerphone was their only connection to this man who could not be seen in person. The telephone would be his lifeline to all of us. He did not want to be recognized outside of his elite circle, which knew him well. That elite circle went all the way up to Hu Jintao.

He spoke to us in Chinese, and to this day I don't know for certain what he said. Uncharacteristic of most Chinese with access to a podium or microphone, he spoke for maybe half an hour, giving people their new marching orders and making it clear that we would follow all of his instructions to a tee. Yoda also praised me lavishly, and assured everyone that we would all be protected. Absolute loyalty was essential. He made it clear that each and every one of us should be willing to sacrifice our lives for this cause. Yoda's credibility throughout China would ensure that our program flourished, and it was ultimately that credibility that made me comfortable in my crucial but restricted role. There was, of course, my new role as a mouthpiece, talking to everybody, anybody I met, about Christianity, Canada, my respect for human life, anything but Pink Pagoda itself. I became the ultimate red herring, hiding in plain sight.

Looking back on my visit to that temple, I realize how much those tiny bundles have taught me. I can't save all the babies in jeopardy; I can't even save most of them. Those I can save offer hope to a tragically sanctioned people whose children are all too often a commodity within political machinations. I can also hope that people who hear about our program, along with those who read this book, will feel a call to action. It's not only about saving babies already at risk; it's about finding a way to stop gendercide altogether.

I am a man on a mission.

15

IS THIS YOUR CHINESE BABY?

Under Yoda's watchful eye, adoptions were in full swing both in China and in North America. The latter were always more complicated and open to scrutiny beyond the Chinese borders where Yoda's network could exercise more control. This next adoption was going to be directly to an American couple, and this time I had become the unwitting Coffee Drinker.

I was at the airport at Qingdao, a hub for flights to Yantai, far-flung regions to the north and northeast, and also to Beijing. Unlike at Western airports, the jets at this airport were covered with netting so that from the air they looked like hills and could not be detected by satellite. The jets were mostly Russian, and there on the runways, one could not distinguish where the runway ended or where the planes began. Such security is not uncommon in other parts of China as well.

Given the extent of my travels throughout China, I frequently used this airport, and this was ironically the second time I had met this particular couple. The first time had been in Hong Kong perhaps a year earlier, and we had exchanged the kind of pleasantries that include promising to call if they were going to be back in China.

"So, Jim, we're coming to China. Will you be anywhere near Qingdao?"

"Yes, I'll actually be passing through there. Let me know when you're arriving and I'll change my plans to spend a couple of hours with you."

Times were coordinated, and I was looking forward to seeing them again. The couple were Chinese Americans; and when I had first seen them at the airport in Hong Kong, I had approached them, speaking to them in my very limited Mandarin. They had looked at me in surprise.

"Whoa, sorry; we may look Chinese, but we're Americans. We don't speak Chinese at all."

I had felt a little silly. Such a typical Western gaffe to presume that someone who looks Chinese must speak Chinese. We all got a good laugh from my blunder, and then the conversation turned to an art gallery we both knew about. From there we somehow segued to the fact that his grandfather was from Hong Kong, and that they were traveling there to see if they could discover some of the history surrounding their family. They were also hoping to be able to adopt a child.

Like most people who come to China in search of a baby or toddler, they were on guard for those adoption agencies that consistently ripped off anxious parents, charging exorbitant amounts of money. They were hoping to find a more reputable agency on the mainland, and there it was.

The man handed me his business card, and I had held on to it. They were a lovely couple, and I had really liked them. They had no idea who I was, and I chose to reveal nothing. Now fate had put them back in my life. I figured God must be sending me a message.

I decided that not only should I meet them; I should also tell them who I was and what I did.

"I need to tell you something about what I do. I changed my plans to meet with you because I was so impressed with you at our first meeting. I think I can help you with your adoption search."

They looked understandably bemused, and I continued.

"How soon do you want to adopt?"

Bemused was looking more like bewildered.

"Well, what exactly do you mean by that?"

They were now looking at me as if to say, "What happened to the guy with the schools? What's this about strange-sounding adoptions?"

I pressed on. I just knew in my heart that these two would make wonderful parents, and God knows I had babies.

"So, tomorrow?"

Bemused to bewildered to maybe just a little bit of *Beware!*

"I won't mislead you. This is absolutely illegal, except for one thing.

All the paperwork will be properly in place, but your adoption number would be phony. And one more thing: it won't cost you a penny."

Move all the way to baffled.

"It would cost us nothing?"

"Yep, that's the deal. I provide you with a baby, and you pay nothing."

What I don't tell them is that I will be taking care of all their expenses. They don't need to know that, a Yoda precaution.

"We're leaving the country in two weeks. You mean we could actually take a baby home with us?"

"Yes. You have one week to let me know what you decide, and in the meantime we need to go make a copy of your passports and any other documents you will entrust to me."

"Whoa."

At least their voices were tinged with laughter. I knew that I was pushed for time, and they had to make some kind of preliminary decision before we parted company. They would have to trust me, much as I had trusted them enough to even raise the question of adopting an "illegal" baby. I also knew that I could mobilize my paperwork people in sufficient time to get everything set up.

"We'll do it."

Like most of the parents with whom we place children, most don't care whether the child is a boy or a girl. Some even request damaged children who might otherwise not be so easily adopted. I've had parents request children with cleft palates. There is a consideration here, however. If we place a child who down the road will need corrective surgery, the parents must take care of that as part of our original agreement. We do track our adoptions, and it would not be unusual for one of our people to make a visit to someone who might have elected to buy a new car instead of fixing the child's deformity. To this day, we know where all of our babies are. Sometimes, it's just a matter of financial hardships that arise. Should that occur, we offer money to the parents to make sure that the baby has the best possible life. Our adoptions do not end at the front door or at the airport. They are forever. We exist to serve the needs of both parents and children, and somehow people who come to us know that.

If you offer, they will come. The adoption business is also my "field of dreams."

Deformities or hardship aside, we also set up an educational fund for each of our adoptees, and some of those funds have yielded as much as 3,000 percent.

Back to my airport couple, they did indeed call me back, and they didn't wait for two weeks. Unfortunately, our calls managed to miss each other; and after three frantic calls to me, they had grown anxious. I assured them that we could still provide them with a baby before they left. What they didn't know was that I had no idea which baby they were going to receive. I would choose whomever was closest, which means that in any given two-week period, there could be twenty-five to forty babies ready to adopt. It's all about the timing.

In addition to timing, we also did our best to match physiognomies, so that facial characteristics were reasonably consistent with those of the parents. We would never give a baby with Mongolian features to a couple from Shanghai.

Facial features were a surprising twist to another adoption story.

I happened to be traveling in the United States, and had gone to one of those gargantuan malls. I was planning to eat in a particular restaurant, but chose instead to wander two floors down from where the restaurant was located. I walked into a sporting goods shop, and happened to notice a couple who then nearly dropped their three-year-old when they saw me.

"Is this one of our Chinese babies?"

The parents looked at me quizzically.

I knew this baby was one of ours, and I was struck by the serendipity and timing required for me to encounter one of them so far from China.

"Aren't you . . . ?"

They couldn't quite recognize my face, but it was clear that I looked familiar to them.

"Yes, I'm Jim Garrow."

Tears on both sides, and I was struck by how far my adoption world extended. We parted company, and I smiled to myself as I walked away. With Min, a sporting goods shop had been a source of pain for both me and her. Here in this mall in the middle of America, a sporting goods shop had offered me peace and a feeling of redemption. For all of us.

God is alive and well in the great malls of America.

16

TO SLEEP PERHAPS
TO DREAM

We'll call him Dr. B. He had been with us for about a year and had been most helpful with medical issues surrounding our babies and children. He was not a hands-on part of the actual transference process; those details were handled by our staff, under Yoda's supervision. Even I did not presume to tell Yoda how to do his job. For whatever reason, arrogance or a strange kind of intransigent meddling, the good doctor quickly and inexplicably went from being just a very good doctor, to an intrusive, self-important, pain in the neck.

This particular adoption was for twins traveling to the United States. A boy and a girl, they were not to be split up during that transfer, and everyone on Yoda's team knew exactly what to do. The doctor insisted that the children must travel separately, Even worse, he was insisting that he have direct contact with the adoptive parents. I didn't find out about this until later, during one of Yoda's debriefing sessions when he would typically give me a summary of activity and a careful accounting of all monies.

The doctor's insistence caused us to go into stealth mode. Yoda concocted a plan worthy of any covert operative.

After the doctor refused to accept that he could not be an active part of the adoption itself, Yoda capitulated and agreed that he could meet the adoptive parents. And meet them he did. Only the couple he met were not the real adoptive parents. The actors assured him that things could be done his way. No way.

It was a case of pure, creative buffoonery. The doctor met a joyful family with a beautiful child. Wrong family, right child.

The additional complication for Yoda's people was that all of this was taking place on American soil. Even today, Yoda's son oversees a huge presence of Chinese operatives in the United States, and also in Canada. For this gambit it was another case, albeit more complicated, of bait and switch.

While the doctor was smug within his delusion that he was in charge, Yoda's people arranged for the twins to travel on a later flight from the one told to the doctor. The destinations were also altered so that it would be impossible for the doctor to intervene. The babies arrived at their destination, together, and the doctor was none the wiser. Afterward we fired him, and I never heard from him again. Someone asked me whether or not something had happened to him. I don't know and I don't want to know.

Not knowing was precisely what helped to keep me safe, along with the babies. I may have been out there in the mix, espousing my views on life and politics, but when it came to Pink Pagoda, I said nothing to the world at large. Yoda had been most clear about that.

"Talk about anything you want; give speeches; tell everyone what you think. Just don't ever use those two words."

In a way, writing this book is a direct violation of Yoda's cardinal rule. In a very real and frightening way, I am no longer hiding in plain sight. With the launch of this book, I will live the rest of my life at risk, along with my family. It is a risk all of us are willing to take.

My only security comes from Yoda's words when we first met.

"You do what I say, and I will protect you."

I choose to believe that he will continue to do that, even in the face of such public scrutiny. His son is aware of this book, and my only injunction has been to "be careful."

I am being careful. True to my Yoda training, all names, places, and operational details have been changed or modified in order to protect our ongoing work. Certainly, the Chinese government is aware of our activities, and I do respect their desire not to be vilified for what has become an entrenched law. In particular, the military, which possibly suffers most at having to relinquish their daughters, continues to work with us in our mission to save China's baby girls. We are not pointing to villains; we are honoring heroes.

People often ask what it was like during those first couple of years after Yoda took over. It was an adventure from the get-go. On any given day, I had no idea who might come walking through my office door. Yoda's people came and went on a regular but unpredictable basis, being careful to explain their specific duties and how I should work with them. And those comings and goings were not confined to my office.

Sometimes, I would get into a cab and be surprised that the driver spoke perfect English. Perfect Yoda.

Other times, I would be walking down the street and someone would bump into me and then keep going. Later on I would discover that there was something for me from Yoda surreptitiously placed in my vest pocket. Or it could be a note from someone else, about a baby or a meeting, or just information I needed to have. Sometimes I did feel a little like James Bond. All I needed was Yoda's signature gun. I have never carried a gun.

Other times, the notes might just be to recommend a good restaurant that I might enjoy. Or someone I should meet. No matter what, Yoda was behind it all.

That transition from the guy in charge to the guy with the checkbook didn't happen overnight. The entire process probably took about six months. During that time, the program grew significantly larger. I know that because the amount of money I was providing grew significantly larger. To date, it is well over $50 million.

The organization also became much more effective, as Yoda had promised it would. Because of his presence in the world of intelligence, everybody was watching everybody else. The scary people were always watching us, and Yoda's people were always watching the scary people. Powerful guanxi kept everything in balance and everyone safe. Yoda also made it a point to set examples and right wrongs.

Shortly after we resolved the problem with the difficult doctor, we found ourselves in the position of becoming what can only be described as avenging angels. I say "we" because I was aware of what happened, but it was not officially a function of Pink Pagoda.

All of us knew that there was and still is a booming trade in human trafficking that operates under the guise of legitimate orphanages. They are anything but legitimate. One in particular was in Chongqing, and was notorious for its role in providing babies and little girls for the sex trade. Girls would be taken in the front door as potential adoptees, and then go right out the back door into special locations where the girls could be raised and trained as sex workers of various types. Some of those girls were actually kept in pens, and when I saw a picture of one of those girls, I could simply not believe that one human being could do that to another. Yoda took that outrage one step further.

Of course, I heard about it later; and once again, I did not ask for particulars. In one day, the entire orphanage was closed, and all of its people gone. When I say gone, I mean they permanently disappeared. An angry Yoda was like the sword of the Lord, smiting all who were sinners. These people were the worst of sinners, and no one, including me, ever asked what happened to them. The babies and children were saved. That was the only justice to focus on.

To my knowledge, that was the only such operation Yoda ever undertook. Much more common was having him show up where I was having dinner, or bumping into him at a bar—after one of his designated cab drivers picked me up from one of my favorite restaurants and then returned me to the site via a side trip. Those meetings were only for sharing information that I needed to get in person. Mostly it was the telephone or clandestine notes. Yoda always knew where I was, what I'd had for dinner. I daresay there wasn't a movement in my life that he didn't monitor.

The last time I saw Yoda, he was in his late seventies. He had retired from his formal position in the military and was focused on transferring power to his son "when the time came." He had been grooming his son since childhood, and by all observations, including Yoda's, his son was and is even smarter. No one said anything to me about Yoda perhaps being ill, but I sensed that something was wrong.

To all appearances, he was having a drink with a woman at the same Qingdao bar as I was. That was most unusual. I had never seen Yoda with a woman before, any woman. This one looked more like a prop, like someone to make him blend in better. To me it just seemed odd. At one point, he walked over to me, shared some not-so-unusual information, and then walked back to his drink and his prop. I finished my Heineken and left. It was the last time I saw him.

After my business in Qingdao was completed, I headed back to

Canada. It was there that Yoda's son got in touch with me to let me know that his father had died. That was two years ago. I have not been back to China since. After the announcement of my Nobel Peace Prize nomination, the Chinese government revoked my passport. In a very sad way, I can never go home again.

Pink Pagoda will never leave.

17

HIS KINGDOM FOR A CAMARO?

Remembering Yoda took me back to those first two years with Pink Pagoda before he arrived on the scene. Back in those early days, I was totally hands-on with our daily operations, wrangling everything from formula to diapers to wet nurses to medical assistance. One of the more surprising things I quickly learned was that not only were there plentiful couples willing to adopt our babies, but that there were couples who wanted to adopt children with birth defects or who were in some way physically challenged. In this particular case, we arranged to save two girls, a newborn and her one-year-old sister. The newborn had a serious, non-life-threatening congenital birth defect, and it only took a few days to identify a couple who was not only willing, but eager to adopt her.

The couple lived in the United States and were part of our rather sophisticated database, which categorized couples according to their preferences for a child. The American couple were in the military, and it was beautifully ironic and also appropriate that the birth parents were also in the Chinese military. Even if the child were going to be raised in the United States, in some small way the military tradition would be upheld. The birth father was especially grateful to know that his daughter would grow up in a military family.

All the arrangements were made, and that included giving specific medical instructions to the new parents. Those instructions also specified when the child would need to have her corrective surgery in order to achieve optimal results. Doctors Without Borders was abundantly generous, helping us not only with the general care of our children, but also with familiarizing parents who were adopting special-needs children with the unusual care their kids would require. The American parents clearly understood and accepted both the physical challenges of their new baby and also the financial responsibility of the surgery. They committed to everything without hesitation.

So, off the baby went to the United States, along with the baby kit that we provided for each of our children. The kits typically had the essential supplies needed for a baby during that first week after the adoption, all nicely packaged in a cloth bag. The bags were made by one of our people, who eventually created a cottage industry out of her ability to sew brilliantly. She quickly went from cloth bags to socks, and employed people from all over her community. That's how businesses start and grow in China, much like those old-fashioned cottage industries that continue to spring up all over North America. Our industrious employee went on to establish plants all over China; today, she is the largest sock manufacturer in the world, and it all started with a simple cloth bag for newborns.

Meanwhile, the baby with the birth defect was happily ensconced with her new family, and in just a couple of years she would be ready to have her corrective surgery. The parents knew the window for that surgery was very narrow, and our tracking associates were keeping a close watch on her progress, unbeknownst to the parents. Although Pink Pagoda tracks all of our adoptees, we pay special attention to families with children needing special care. Word quickly reached me while I was traveling in the United States that our military baby was now a toddler and that the parents had not yet made the necessary arrangements. I thought at first that perhaps they were having financial difficulties, and asked my associate if that was the issue.

"So, do we need to send them money?"

I was more than willing to help out, if that was what would be required for the surgery to take place, and the parents already knew that.

"No, Dr. Jim, they haven't asked for any money. In fact, they just bought a new Corvette; and we're concerned that the money for that car really should have been used for the baby's surgery."

I went from pink to red. Unfortunately for the parents, I also just happened to be traveling a few miles from where the couple lived. I jumped into my rental car and wondered as I drove how these people could put the pleasure of a new car over their daughter's health.

As I neared their home, I realized that I should have seen a red flag when the couple didn't ask for financial assistance as the time for the surgery approached. All adoptive parents are told to ask if they need anything, and that includes financial help. My associate also told me that the couple had borrowed the money for their new car from one of those expensive loan companies that can easily double the cost of the car over time. Time for a little debt resolution.

I arrived at their home and knocked on the front door. They didn't recognize me, so I introduced myself.

"Hello. I'm Dr. James Garrow, and we need to talk."

They escorted me into the living room, we all sat down, and as they do in those old Western films, I proceeded to read to them from the good book.

"You can either set this straight or face exposure."

The nature of the exposure was obvious. I would turn them in to the authorities for securing an illegal adoption, and I would also take back the child. His military career would be over, and there could potentially be criminal charges against both of them. My Dad taught me how to bluff quite well!

"No, no, Dr. Garrow," the mother said. "We'll take care of this right away. I am so sorry. My husband had his heart set on that new car, and, well, it was just stupid on our part. We love our little girl, and we'll do whatever you tell us to do."

The husband sat there quietly, shamed by his wife's words, but I couldn't help noticing that he was glancing out the window to where the Corvette was parked. The next day, the husband returned the car, and I offered to help defray the cost of the operation. Today, that little girl is probably about eight, and her health is a ten.

Back in China, we continued to rescue babies with physical problems, and our associates continued to battle emotional issues for all of those children, healthy or not. Thank God for the woman who reminded me so much of Mother Teresa.

Our Chinese counterpart to that sainted woman was approximately sixty-five when she joined our organization, and right away she became like the Great Mother overseeing our associates. From the beginning, we realized that one of our challenges would be protecting our people from their own emotions. At first, associates who were taking care of babies while they waited for adoptive parents would become attached to those children and want to adopt them. Emotionally, our people needed guidance and counseling about the work they were doing, and our Great Mother became the ultimate counselor, mentoring our associates until they "caught it." Not taught, but caught. It's a Scottish expression that captures perfectly how the people she mentored caught what she was offering.

Hope and loss, hope and loss. Those were her key principles. She also taught our people how to care for children with special needs, like babies with cleft palates, who required special feeding techniques. Remarkably, she even taught our wet nurses how to properly suckle those babies. She also oversaw our verbal lines of communication within the organization, making sure that critical care information regarding babies made its way to the right people. I thought of it as our verbal manual; nothing written down, but thorough and well organized.

Even with all of our Great Mother's best efforts, we did lose people along the way. The emotional stress was just too much for them. For those who stayed on, their financial future was bright, including retirement when they were older. When I left China for the last time, our Great Mother was nearly seventy-five and getting ready to retire. In that regard, she was unlike Mother Teresa, who worked up until the time of her death. I actually met Mother Teresa when I went to India. Not only did I meet her; I also shook her hand—actually, both hands. Those hands were not at all what I expected. They were strong, and I swear they were the size of meat cleavers. The Great Mother's hands were like that, too. Hers were the hands of someone who had worked hard in the fields before joining our organization, and the last time I held them, it was to present her with a special certificate from the Bethune Institute, thanking her for all her years of dedication and hard work with our associates and our babies. The Chinese people love certificates, and she was so grateful for the honor that she literally squeezed my hands until they hurt. In that moment, I was transported back to Calcutta, and to the woman whose "certificate" to me was a signed postcard commemorating a special visit by Pope John XXIII. For years I treasured that postcard, and then I donated it to *Crisis* magazine when I attended the gala celebrating their new office building in Washington, D.C. I had paid an exorbitant amount of money to have it beautifully framed, and I have no doubt that with Mother Teresa's death, the value of the postcard would have been extraordinary. It wasn't about the value. Mother Teresa was part of the Catholic Church, and it was fitting that the signed postcard reside with Catholics. All I have left is a picture of me and the postcard, which is still on my website.

For the Great Mother, I have only memories, along with the satisfaction of knowing that we paid for her grandson to attend college in the United States. I've had a very rich life.

18

THE WILD RIDE

Back here in Canada, my adventures are much tamer than those in my past. From the time I was very young, I have traveled to interesting places because I was compelled to find out "where" and when possible, "why."

After reading about such places when I was too young to travel, my young adult years began an ongoing odyssey to visit the places I had only seen in print. I went to Westminster Abbey so I could see where Queen Elizabeth was buried. With Lord Mountbatten of Burma, I was intrigued by both his life and the manner of his death—he was killed by a bomb planted on his boat by the IRA. I knew that he had been buried under the floor of Romsey Abbey in Britain, and of course I had to go there. Given my Scottish heritage, I also had to visit Bannockburn in the Scottish Highlands in order to see the famous battlefield there. While most people were content to learn about William Wallace in the Mel Gibson movie *Braveheart*, I had to see where the battle really happened.

My curiosity extended to the bizarre as well. I had to travel to London to see where Jack the Ripper killed all those girls. In contrast, I also hired a guide to show me the classrooms at Oxford where famous personalities had conducted classes. For me, the spirit of an event is steeped in the place where that event occurred. When I'm in such places, I also sense things.

Now, I realize there might be those who think I'm a bit off. Typically, people who "sense" things are considered part of the lunatic fringe, or judged by those whose religious beliefs make such things at least a little suspect.

I am neither a psychic nor a medium. I just feel things in a way that somehow brings me closer to that particular person or event. All of us have experienced that at one time or another, walking into a room where the energy is just "off," or very positive. I think perhaps my voracious reading habits have simply inclined me to better connect with people and places. Nothing more.

So, when I got into that cab in Qingdao for the three-hour trip to Yanti, where was my sense of person and place?

Yoda had always said that the most improbable things had a way of finding me. When I arrived at the airport, all of the flights had been cancelled because of a major electrical storm. Typhoon weather is one of the banes of living in China, and that bane was now about to prevent me from getting to a speaking engagement on behalf of my schools.

Even if I'd tried to get back to Chongqing, there weren't buses or any form of transportation that went directly to Yanti, which is far up the coast and way off the beaten track.

There I was, standing in the pouring rain, thinking while I got drenched, when up walked a guy, directly in front of me.

"Taxi? Need taxi?"

"No, no thanks."

I didn't think a taxi would take me where I needed to go, but I'm never rude to people.

"We take you anywhere, cheap-cheap."

"Anywhere?"

I was both incredulous and skeptical. All I could think of was that ad with the devil where the guy in need of transportation says, "Anywhere?" I wasn't about to get in a strange cab with a potential devil.

But then that "What the heck?" Jim Garrow took over.

"Well, I have to go to Yanti."

"Oh, no problem, no problem."

He took me and my bags out to a waiting taxi, and started up a dialogue with the driver. I didn't understand a word; I just sat there and waited for my trip to begin.

Heading out on the devil's highway.

We drove for a while on the main highway, then pulled over at an overpass, where five, maybe ten, taxis were all lined up, just sitting there, the drivers yakking away, and here comes this Chinese guy with a white passenger. One of the drivers, who looked to be the boss and who spoke a bit of English, walked over to our cab and started talking to my driver. I noticed he had a wad of cash in his hand.

"So, you want to go to Yanti?"

Now I felt more like the female novelist in the movie *Romancing the Stone*, starring Kathleen Turner and Michael Douglas.

"So, you want to go to Cartagena?"

The question had a distinct twist to it.

"Yeah," I said.

"That will cost you three hundred kwai."

He was acting as if that might be a lot of money for me to pay; in reality it's more like fifty dollars, which for a three-hour cab trip is nothing.

"Sure, I'll pay that."

By now, I was outside, standing next to the cab, while my driver and the boss were discussing something I couldn't understand.

"Okay, you get in that cab."

The driver carefully loaded not only my suitcase, but also my backpack, laptop, and projector for doing presentations at my speaking engagement. I settled into my new cab; and while I thought this a bit strange, I was not really afraid. The boss walked over to the cab and put his head inside the window.

"Do not leave the cab."

Why would I want to leave the cab?

"Do not leave the cab."

"Why would I leave the cab?"

I didn't really expect an answer; it was more like thinking out loud.

"No matter what. It may look like he's not taking you where you want to go, but he is. Sometimes, we have to use back roads, back roads many times."

Now I was thinking to myself, not out loud. *What in the world? Are the roads washed out up ahead? What other reason . . . ?* Time for out loud.

"Why do you have to use back roads? Why do you have to dodge around?"

Dodge was definitely not the right word.

"We do nothing illegal, nothing illegal!"

Now I was nervous, because it was becoming clear to me that he *was* doing something illegal.

We took off, devil at the wheel and victim in the backseat. We traveled nearly three hours, and our destination was still some time away. I really couldn't tell, because I didn't know those back roads, but I did recognize that up ahead was a police checkpoint. My driver responded in a heartbeat and took off on a different road, down a ditch and onto a little trail that went up over a hill. I remember thinking to myself, *There's no way this car will make it on that trail,* but it did, and then there was another one. The driver then went way past the checkpoint before getting back on the highway.

Even though there were no other cars on this major, four-lane highway, I wasn't worried. There are many such roads throughout China where you will see no other cars. Most Chinese can't afford automobiles, but areas get federal monies to build roads, so here we were, with miles and miles of no cars. New roads mean new buildings, and that means profit for someone, but probably not the Chinese peasant who can't afford a vehicle.

Was I scared? Not at all. I had my cell phone with me, and I was in range to reach someone if I needed help. The real reason for my calm demeanor was Yoda. Yoda's influence and guanxi reaches out to even the most remote places and to the most common taxi driver. I had no doubt that Yoda probably knew exactly where I was, and I'm guessing he was having a good chuckle over it.

Before we finally reached our destination in Yantai, we had a couple more dodges, but after the first one I just settled back and got into the spirit of the ride. Later on, Yoda would tell me that I was lucky they were on their way to a drug exchange, and that I was going to the right place and would pay them for the ride. I was a mule without a mission, just a guy coming along for the ride.

When I got to Yantai, I checked into my hotel and settled into the comfort of my room. I echoed Michael Douglas's words in that same movie, when he finally arrives safely in Cartagena after enduring an adventure to get there.

"This is nice."

19

AMERICA, COAST TO COAST

B ack when I was eighteen, it was "flower children" who pulled me back toward the United States. It was the summer of love, and I wanted to get into the American groove.

Thanks to my businesses and investments, I didn't have to worry about money for the trip. I also had a gold credit card, a rarity at that time, and knew that I would have access to my money back in Canada whenever I needed it. My plan was to hitchhike for most of the trip, because I wanted to experience as many different kinds of people as I possibly could. I also wanted to visit those historical places that intrigued me, along with discovering new sites. It was time for a walkabout.

One of my intentional destinations was the Ford Theater, where Lincoln was shot. Not just the theater, the actual box that Lincoln was sitting in. I managed to sneak in, and made my way to the box. Since I was a child, I have always somehow felt "presences" in certain places, and here in this theater I truly felt the presence of the man who had died here. Not his spirit in any conventional sense, but in the sense of being connected to his anima through the wood, fabric, and dust of the building. I felt as though I were part of an American tragedy, and I felt a kinship with American patriotism. All throughout my trip I saw patriotism that was genuinely heartfelt, so often steeped in the blood of those who were currently dying in the Vietnam War, and those who had died long before. That patriotism had a profound impact on me; and while I have been known to jokingly refer to the United States as "the Excited States of America," I didn't feel that way as I moved among its people and landmarks.

Things that don't happen regularly to most people happen to me, especially when I travel. Just recently I had been in Britain, and was drawn to the Beefeater guards who stand in front of Buckingham Palace. Everyone knows they're not allowed to talk to anyone. That didn't stop me from asking.

"Where's the Queen mum's place?" I asked one of the guards.

We looked at each other, both acknowledging the decorum of the situation.

"Look, I'm Canadian; nobody's around. Where's the Queen mum's place?"

His lips never moved, but the words were clear.

"Up the street, Saint James."

I swear, his lips never moved. It was marvelous. Here was this guy, under strict orders never to utter a word, but he did so for me. That's how it always is with me. Before Britain, before China, and all the way back to my walkabout—and even before that—special things happened to me. Many times I didn't even have to ask. All I had to do was show up.

The battlefield at Gettysburg was an example of that. There I was, barely eighteen, with longish hair and looking a lot like "one of those hippies." I was leaning against a cannon, eating a banana. A man who looked to be around eighty walked up to me and inquired if I was going to put the peel in a nearby wastebasket.

"Sir, I would never dishonor this place by dropping garbage."

My response stopped him in his tracks, and he asked me if I knew much about this place.

"Well, I'm not sure if you can tell, but I'm not an American; I'm Canadian. I'd love to know more about this place."

And with that he began to regale me with Civil War stories about different battles, and General Sherman, and the march through Savannah, and just so many things I would never have known. We stayed there for hours, and I was so grateful. All because of a banana peel. Or was it?

As I made my way across the country, there were other "wonders." The Lincoln Memorial, where I discovered much to my surprise that the two sides of Lincoln's face are not the same. One shows his youth, the other his aged visage. I found myself with my own personal tour guide, who shared more than I could have expected from a standard tour guide. This fellow just came and talked with me. Then there was this beautiful old church in a rural part of South Carolina where the caretaker volunteered to take me on a special tour. And of course, hanging out at an Oregon airport with the legendary Taj Mahal, the two of us sitting on the floor, waiting for the fog to clear, he rehearsing for an upcoming concert, me just sitting there taking it all in. We sat there for hours, absorbed in the music, just the two of us.

All across America I hitched rides with truckers, vacationing families, businesspeople, young kids like me, all manner of characters. I had absorbed America through all of my senses, and I was enriched by the experience. Years later I would return to conduct business transactions with then governor of Texas George Bush. I would not be negotiating as a foreigner, not entirely. I had partaken of the American spirit, and the sense of what it is to be an American.

China wouldn't be far beyond.

20

A CANADIAN YANKEE
IN HU JINTAO'S
COURT

The invitation to come to China for the first time produced a whirlwind of new people and guided tours of every significant attraction that my guides could think of. The day after the extravagant banquet in my honor, I found myself being picked up at the Hilton Hotel where I was staying, and escorted to my waiting car. That second day is when I began to see China with very different eyes from my initial view.

That morning I had only had to walk from the front door of the hotel to my car, and it felt as though I had walked into a sauna with the heat turned up to unbearable. By the time I closed the car door behind me, I was soaked in sweat from my very few steps in the 125.6-degree heat. That is not an exaggeration; and anyone who has been to Chongqing or a comparable big city will attest to the fact that temperatures can soar well over 100. This particular day was a record for the largest city in the world, and poor people were literally dying by the hundreds.

The city of Chongqing sits in a bowl of mountains at the confluence of the Yangtze and Jialing rivers. The term "dry heat" has no application in this topography. One course of the waters is heavy with silt, and snakes its way into the clear mountain runoff just over the bank from the area known as Jai Fong Bai. This is the ultimate heat sink, with nary a breeze to disturb the air, thus polluting the atmosphere with a particulate matter register of six times that of New York City. What was to become my office in Chongqing was hidden in the cliffs overlooking the river, and was one of the most famous "holes" in all of China. Chou En-lai had hidden out in my particular hole when the Japanese overran the city and murdered more than five hundred thousand Chinese people. That brutality has never been forgotten, and the phrase I heard so often—"one day"—illustrates the simmering need for revenge felt by the Chinese. Like Tony Soprano, who said that revenge is a dish best served cold, China, it was clear, though belied by their presently cool emotions, sees a special banquet in their future. It reminded me never to alienate a Chinese person. Unlike Westerners whose memories tend to be short, the Chinese think not only years ahead, but generations ahead. This is one of the reasons why anyone who truly wants to understand the Chinese mentality must also embrace the importance of relationships whose influence may reach far into the future.

Food seems to be one of the more common ways to develop and nurture those relationships.

As most people traveling or living in a foreign country know, one of the first things one looks for is the best places to eat. Chinese restaurants were expectedly prolific, along with a Korean restaurant in Chongqing that I especially liked. But my sights were set on a hotel that offered excellent Western fare. It was located outside the main city, and catered to local and high-ranking military officials who saw the restaurant as their private club. Translation: white foreigners not welcome. They didn't know Jim Garrow, yet.

I showed up at the restaurant, in full view of all the military brass seated in this very large restaurant, and waited inside the front door to be seated. My translator was along for the quest, and the manager made it very clear that I was not welcome here. My translator responded by explaining that I was an extremely wealthy school owner from China, with guanxi right up to the highest government levels. That got me a seat, not in the main restaurant, but outside in the spacious hotel lobby, while inquiries were made about me. Of course this was pre-Yoda, but I still had significant guanxi connections. The maître d' came over and asked for both my passport and any supporting documents, which he then whisked away to a table in the back of the restaurant, where a group of brass was scrutinizing me from afar. In the meantime, everyone in this room of nearly four hundred people had stopped talking and eating. The fact that I was not an American seemed to assure them that I was not a spy; now it would be up to my documents to reveal just how high up my guanxi extended. Ultimately, I was allowed to stay and eat, albeit alone in a small dining room off to the side of the main dining room. The French doors were closed behind me, and I could hear the hubbub of noise and chatter resume.

Here in my private space, a large television hung from the wall, and I quickly turned it to the only English-speaking station available here. My translator helped me choose food from the menu, and also explained the wine list to me. I'm a great fan of Australian wines, and I ordered a special bottle of Australian cabernet sauvignon to be delivered to the general who had so intently scrutinized my documents. I also asked that the translator give specific wording to the manager who would deliver my gift. When I finished eating, I told the manager that I would return the next day for lunch, and for every day thereafter, and that I would expect to be seated again in my little room. When I left the restaurant, I could see that the bottle of wine was sitting unopened at the general's table. I turned toward him and offered a slight bow, an appropriate gesture of manners and respect.

I did indeed return the next day, and by the fifth day there was a breakthrough. Really, it was an opportune visit to the washroom, where one of the officers ended up standing next to me. He spoke English, and let me know that while the general had appreciated the gesture of the red wine, it was grappa that he preferred. Talk about leaking information.

I invited the officer to join me at my table the next day, and added that I had my private pilot's license from Canada and would show it to him then. I also told him that I owned my own plane, and it was clear that common ground was being established between not only me and the officer but also between the general and me. It's all about the timing.

The next day I phoned a contact in Hong Kong and asked him to send me by courier a case of the best grappa money could buy. I had no idea that this Italian specialty was so expensive, and I nearly choked at the astronomical cost. The next day I brought the case with me to the hotel, and the grappa caper was on. Not only did the general enjoy my largesse; he began sharing the grappa with the other seven officials at his table. More glasses, more guanxi.

By week three, my entry into the restaurant had no impact on the noise and chatter. My pilot's license and a picture of my plane were passed all over the room, and I couldn't calculate guanxi fast enough. Six months later, after a brief time away traveling to my other schools throughout China, I returned to the restaurant and was enthusiastically greeted by the manager, who informed me that the second case of grappa I had dropped off was in need of replenishment. Expensive restocking, but worth every renminbi. I had now insinuated myself into the top military ranks, and I knew that I had accomplished a major coup. Coup de grappa.

21

OF TEA AND
TRANSPORTATION

For all of my times in China, transportation always seemed to offer me some of my best opportunities for adventure. It all started with a need for diapers and formula for the babies I was rescuing early in my mission, but went on to include a luxurious riverboat and a private turbine prop plane used not only for the transportation of babies from one province to another, but also to help deliver supplies to victims of the great Szechuan earthquakes.

My first transportation feat involved feeding and diapering. Newborn babies in particular use up vast quantities of both commodities. We were fortunate in finding a few wet nurses in the beginning weeks of our adoption business, but it soon became apparent that we needed to obtain formula.

Back when we first started, formula was not widely available in China. It wasn't that it couldn't be found at all, but certainly not in the quantities we were going to need. To further complicate things, the formula that was currently available could only be purchased through an apothecary. Two tasks: find formula in large batches and find a place to dispense it.

I managed to find the product I needed in the United States. I also found a diaper supplier there as well. Now the issue was transportation. The cost would be exorbitant. What to do?

Through one of my contacts in China, I found out that cargo ships go back and forth between the United States and China on a regular basis. America was and is consuming mass quantities of Chinese-made goods, and the ocean had become a superhighway of commerce. After the ships disembarked and unloaded their goods in the States, they returned empty to China, there to be restocked with more goods. Some might see an empty vessel; I saw a full cargo hold.

I negotiated with the shipping company and convinced them to come back to China with our desperately needed supplies. It was one of the rare occasions where something we needed for Pink Pagoda didn't cost me a fortune. We were now set up to properly feed and diaper our babies. Except for one thing. The milk run.

We still needed an apothecary to handle distribution. Once again, my growing guanxi found us a woman whose business would be perfect. A deal was struck, and the milk started to flow.

Commodities were the simplest of my transportation challenges. We could also move our people via plane, train, bus, or taxi. The biggest challenge soon became the babies themselves.

While we had been managing to handle all of our transporting with standard forms of travel, it was the deaths of two of our people that led Yoda and me to consider a safer venue that was also faster and more dependable. The two employees who had been victimized during an exchange would have been safe if they hadn't had to depend upon local sources to handle that exchange. Much as I would like to say more, I truly can't. Suffice it to say that both Yoda and I were devastated, and I resolved to find a solution that would keep everyone out of harm's way.

What we needed was an airplane.

My goal was to find an organization that already had a plane and work out an arrangement with them. I contacted the manufacturer of the plane I wanted and asked them where I could find one close by, or for that matter, anywhere in China. He told me that he knew of only one in all of Asia. I only needed one.

I made my proposal to the manufacturer.

"What I'd like to do is buy part, or even all, of your plane and then lease it back to you. The deal would be that when I needed the plane, I could use it, kind of like a time-share with wings."

I don't know that he appreciated my humor, but he got the gist of what I wanted. He contacted the owner, and the deal was struck. I ended up buying the entire plane, and then set about putting together a crew of Canadian pilots and assorted crew members. I was now in the airplane business.

The plane itself would remain stationed in Bangkok, Thailand, because that is the depot for making engine repairs and performing maintenance service. My plane is a Pilatus PC-12 with a Pratt & Whitney turbine engine, and requires type A jet fuel, the kind used by commercial jets. Everything the plane needed to stay in top flying condition and stay fueled was in Bangkok. The plane is intended for twelve people; however, with a club configuration, the plane would more comfortably accommodate six people, two pilots, and a stewardess. We were not running a baby club.

Without much difficulty, the plane could handle fifteen bassinets and a handful of assistants, but there was one occasion where we had twenty-two. That was an emergency scenario, and that one aside, we typically averaged six babies and never exceeded fifteen. Babies would be dropped off at locations all over China, and air travel provided for a much quicker, safer transport for everyone.

When the earthquakes hit Szechuan in 2007, medical supplies were desperately needed at mobile medical units and makeshift hospitals. The problem was that no one trusted the Chinese to deliver those goods, and Chinese officials turned to the Canadians. And me.

"Absolutely."

I didn't hesitate for an instant, and for three full months my plane and crew were at the beck and call of the Chinese military, which was coordinating the relief mission across the province. My plane was ideal, first because it was small enough to get into smaller areas, and also because the rear of the plane could accommodate a loaded fork lift pallet in a large door on the port side of the plane.

For the brief interludes between those missions of mercy, the planes were at the disposal of high-ranking military officials. That luxury served to substantially increase my guanxi. The more guanxi I had, the more protected I and my people would be. That was the best $4 million I ever spent.

Not all modes of transportation were built around my business needs, but somehow guanxi was always involved.

Early in my baby rescue missions, I decided I needed to go for a long walk down along the banks of the Yangtze. My good friend and associate, Joe, offered to come with me, and off we went on a pedestrian adventure. Only it turned out not to be pedestrian at all.

There, along the river banks, a profusion of smaller and larger boats are moored. Many people lived on their boats; others simply used them for pleasure. The one that caught our attention that evening definitely looked like a pleasure abode.

We walked down the dock to get a closer look. All along the river, firework displays were starting up, and this was one the big enticements to take a walk along the river's banks. Certainly, we have fireworks back in Canada, and the United States puts on some spectacular displays. Nothing comes close to what the Chinese orchestrate.

While I don't know precisely the cost required to put on such dramatic shows, I do know that for the viewer it is nothing less than celestial magnificence. The sky literally explodes with a rainbow of stars and shoots and blasts, each more amazing than the last. These are not holiday displays; these happen all the time. Given the contrast of the coffee-colored river and the green hills just beyond its waters, the eyes blink in both disbelief and wonderment.

Joe and I were in the mood for a little wonder; what we didn't expect was psychedelic tea.

The riverboat we had walked down to see was perhaps two hundred feet long, and elegantly decked out. Without being intrusive, we took a peek inside. Barely into our peek, the owner came out and invited us to come up on the top deck and join him for tea, while we all watched the fireworks. I wasn't really that surprised, Since I had arrived in China, this kind of thing had continued to happen to me. Complete strangers would walk up to me and stare, or start talking to me. Many had said, sometimes through a translator, that they believed I was the reincarnation of Dr. Norman Bethune. That name again. First, in a high school research project, and now in China all these years later.

Joe wasn't surprised, either. Since he had begun working with me in my Chinese schools, he had experienced firsthand that kind of reception, and it no longer surprised him.

"That's just Jim."

So here we were, being hosted by a stranger who turned out to be a very powerful general, and whose taste in tea ran to extreme connoisseur. I consider myself a tea enthusiast, but I had never seen most of these teas, nor had Joe. The one I finally selected was one of the general's recommendations, and I sipped it languorously, enjoying the fireworks as we drank and talked. The tea was smooth, but with a certain brightness. Even the fireworks seemed brighter than when we had sat down, and I thought it must be the combination of good company and great tea. Joe was watching me with an amused smile, that smile proportionate to the amount I was drinking. I knew that some teas have "mood-enhancing" qualities, and this one seemed to be one of those.

"Jim, are you all right?"

Apparently, my eyes were dancing along with the sparkling lights. It wasn't that I was hallucinating because of how bright the lights were; I was hallucinating, period.

The effects of the tea began to wear off, and eventually, Joe and I thanked our host profusely and headed back to our hotel. It had been a very special evening, and the only transportation I had to think about now was my feet. Those worked just fine, and one could truly say that I ended the evening on a high note.

That, and with a cupful of guanxi.

22

DOUBLE TRAGEDY

Not every baby landed safely in the arms of her new parents.

One of the Coffee Drinkers in a rather remote province had been doing an excellent job finding babies and helping finalize adoptions. She came from a very well-connected family, and worked in tandem with her boyfriend. Both were devoted, conscientious associates, and they were definitely rising in our organizational ranks. They were keenly aware that the first structural move once a baby had been identified was to put together a fail-safe plan so everyone would be protected. We always had a story, a sidebar, and an alternate plan in case anything went wrong. This was the wisdom and brilliance of Yoda, who orchestrated layer upon layer of "what if?" maneuvers. Typically, there were four such layers, and we had not yet encountered a situation where the layers failed to work. Perhaps it was inevitable, but the incident involving these two associates caught us completely off guard, and we were devastated.

The little town where the delivery was to take place was much like many of those small towns throughout China that have been developed around meandering roads that are more like dirt-packed goat paths. There are no grids in the hinterlands. Built up around those meandering paths would be both residences and businesses. On that particular day, the destination was one of the town's main gathering places, a pub where visitors could learn how to brew beer and visit with other people in the town. It was a busy place, and there would be dozens and dozens of people around. No one, certainly not our adoption people, would stand out from anyone else. The new parents would be waiting to meet with our two associates and receive their new baby. Additionally, there was a major festival taking place that day to celebrate a local deity, so the area in which the pub was located was truly bustling with people and activity. There may have been numerous people for safe cover, but the two associates never reached the safety of the pub.

It was and still is well-known that the Chinese Mafia is exceedingly active in the human trafficking trade, and babies are a prime commodity. No one will ever know how the details about that meeting were obtained, but Mafia members intercepted the two associates and the baby they were carrying. The men slit the associates' throats, and stole the baby.

As best could be reconstructed by the person who found their bodies, the two had been coming out of a hall on their way to a waiting vehicle that would take them the rest of the way to where the new parents were waiting. The vehicle itself was one of those antiquated, diesel-spewing contraptions that looks like a cross between a cart and a mini flatbed truck. The front part of the vehicle would accommodate four people, and the back bed was for hauling potatoes or whatever else needed to be transported. When the two associates never reached their destination, our associates waiting for them at the delivery point contacted us. The local police had already been called by the young girl who found their bodies. To use a cliché, we now had a situation on our hands.

Not only had our two associates been killed and our baby stolen, but now we would have to deal with the shock and reactions from the people in this small town where nothing of this type had ever happened before. We would also have to deal with the new parents whose baby was now gone. Then we would have to handle the birth parents, who had entrusted us with their baby. We would also have to handle the parents of the two associates. Beyond that, we would have to deal with the possibility of the townspeople turning us in to the local public security bureau and eventually higher authorities. Yoda was mobilized within minutes, first with damage control and then on to the avenging sword.

First, he brought in the proverbial big guns to squelch any grumblings in the town. Along with the big guns came lots of cash to everyone who might pose a problem, including the parents, both adoptive and birth. Then Yoda put out the word through everyone who at any level had any dealings with our operation.

"If you ever do such a thing again, if you steal one of our children or cause the death of anyone in our organization, you will be dead. Not just you, but everyone in your family and everyone you know."

Those were not idle words.

And to our staff: "If they use a knife on you, use a gun on them. If they use a gun . . ." And the escalation would have no limits.

Nor did Yoda's controlled and focused rage have any limits. Various newspapers picked up the story, and certainly helped to spread Yoda's "good word."

I was back home in Canada when I got the *bad* word from Yoda.

My office was tucked into the far end of our kitchen, and I was just sitting there, looking out onto the pool and barn beyond. I had just taken a lunch break, and was about to enjoy a quesadilla when the phone rang. A call from China could only mean one person, Yoda, and it was midnight in China.

"Jim, two of our people have been killed."

I was shocked and sickened when he told me about the murders, and my bucolic scene disappeared into a vision of two slit throats and a baby in mortal danger. I listened over the next twenty minutes as he painstakingly walked me through what had occurred, down to the last excruciating detail. Finally.

"Can you come?"

I was to fly directly to Beijing, something I had never done before. There was a good reason for that. Whenever I flew in and out of places, Yoda always arranged for a rather serpentine itinerary, whether it was for me or for one of his people. Flying directly was a huge departure from his normal operations, and it only served to heighten my anxiety. The only seat left was in first class and I took it. How ironic, first class for a first-class disaster.

I would be in the air for slightly more than thirteen hours on the first leg of the journey, and I doubted that I would get much sleep. I knew that while I was comfortable in first class, Yoda's people would be dropping out of planes and helicopters all over China, rooting out anyone in the

Chinese Mafia whose hand had in any way touched the event. I suppose one could say that he would find out where all the bodies were buried, except that he hadn't buried them yet.

Before I left, I wrote a quick note with no explanations for my wife. "I had to book a ticket for China. Don't know when I'll be back." Or if.

On the way to the airport, I could not hold back the tears. Even though I hadn't known these two associates personally, they were part of my life, my fabric, my mission. When I arrived in Beijing, there was a file waiting for me. The file contained everything about the two associates' lives. I would need those details because the reason for my coming to China was to meet with both sets of parents. I had no idea what I might say to any of them, but I trusted in God to help me find the right words.

There would be two more flights before I arrived at my destination to meet the parents of the first associate, the man, who had died. The second flight would be by helicopter, for security reasons. My feet would not touch a road until I arrived at the parents' home. Twenty-seven hours had elapsed from the time I disembarked in Beijing until I arrived at their home. Exhaustion was not an option.

My helicopter flight actually involved three copters and roughly 15 people per helicopter. I had more protective coverage than Hu Jintao. That's not hyperbole, just fact. Yoda wasn't among them, but his control was.

The father of the murdered man already knew I was the head of the organization. My coming to see him would be equivalent to having Bill Gates traveling halfway around the world to offer his condolences. I wasn't there just to express condolences; I was coming to verbally and physically accept responsibility for the death of a son. All I could think of was my own son so close to death so many years earlier. My tears now were both for the boy whom God had saved and the one I could not.

23

MY KINGDOM FOR A
HANDKERCHIEF

I arrived at the parents' home, and the sight of this man on his knees
in front of me brought me to tears that I could not stop. Around the
two of us were men setting up chairs for us, Yoda's men, the wife, and
the translator. The translator was a man, very important for etiquette.
When the father finally sat down on one of the chairs, my composure
began to return, and I expressed my shock and outrage about what had
happened, and what an honor it was to have worked with his son. Because
I'd already carefully read the son's file, I could be very specific about the
details, and I think it helped convey my sincerity to his father. I also knew,
although it was not directly shared, that large sums of cash had been
given to anyone in the son's family who might be in need of anything.
That wasn't of concern to me right now. Just this man in front of me, his
wife silent throughout the entire meeting. Her silence was almost worse
than all of the tears.

We concluded, and Yoda's men spirited me away to our next meeting.
This one would be with the woman's mother; her father was deceased.
Having just seen a man on his knees and so remarkably grateful for my
coming to visit him in person, I found the mother at this home shock-
ingly different.

In a word, this woman's emotional level could only be described as
sterile. This time, I was not in a home out in the country; I was booked

into the big-city hotel where the mother worked. The group of individuals accompanying me was large enough to convey my rank in the organization. We also had two uniformed people—Yoda's, of course—and this was the first time I had ever seen anyone in uniform participate in anything we did. There was much conversation, but much of it was never translated for me. The nonverbal communication needed no translation.

The man's father had grabbed and kissed both my hands, thanking me through his tears for having honored his son. This woman just sat there, nearly motionless and the epitome of standoffishness. I wondered if perhaps it was because she was in shock over the death of her daughter. Regardless, her steely exterior caused me a different kind of grief. More sublimated, more unsure.

On the surface, the woman thanked me for coming to the place where the two had been killed, for coming to her city, for booking into her hotel, for agreeing to meet with her, for including her relatives in this meetings. All very perfunctory, all very polite. But missing something. What was it?

I tried to imagine being a woman, widowed, whose daughter, from whom she was estranged for whatever reason, had suddenly been killed. What did that mean to a mother whose daughter had not been on speaking terms with her?

If I imagined myself first as a mother, even with an estranged or difficult relationship with my daughter, who is now meeting the man whose organization is de facto responsible for my daughter's death, what would I think?

I think I, too, would say thank you for this and thank you for that, because if I truly touched my grief in front of the man who had at least some liability for my daughter's death, how would I respond? Would I scream at him in Chinese, whose vitriol could only be communicated through my volume and register? Would I strike out at him physically, pounding my small fists against his chest?

She could do none of those things. To confront me or her emotions in any way would bring about her collapse. I had walked away from the man on his knees feeling somehow exonerated. I left this meeting with my guts hanging out, and there was no Dr. Bethune to save me.

There were other meetings, but post reflection they've become gentle blurs. Gentle, because God has chosen to spare me the additional pain.

Thank you, God.

My final meeting would be with the birth parents of the stolen baby. Now, and maybe for the first time, I came up against the emotions of the father whose decision to set aside his daughter had culminated in her abduction into, most likely, the sex trade.

From the moment he met me he hated me. He and his wife already had a girl. This decision had to take excruciating to an emotional level that I can't even begin to imagine. For reasons I cannot share, this couple would not be allowed to move forward with having a son. I may not be a fan of Jean-Paul Sartre, but this was by any definition, "*Huis Clos*." No exit.

The mother hated me beyond the words she would not share. Not only had she and her husband made the eviscerating decision to give up their daughter, beyond the original decision to have her set aside; they now had to live with the potential reality of their baby girl becoming some lecherous man's plaything.

I tried to think of Xinyi's sister, grief struck at losing her infant daughter on the one hand, but also grateful and relieved to hand her off to a new, loving family on the other. I longed to be back in that stark white apartment, with that sour smell of breast milk and no baby to be nurtured by it. I would have even embraced the acrid smell of cabbage.

The husband looked at me as I apologized profusely. If he had held a dagger in his hands, I would have been dead. At that moment, I almost felt, deservedly so. What had I been thinking? Did I really believe that just because God smiled upon my work, I was exempt from the vagaries of man? What about Yoda? I knew he was out there putting out fires that might conflagrate our beloved Pink Pagoda. I was alone, again.

"I realize that you don't know me, but I am a man who will move heaven and earth to make this right. We will find your daughter, and we will punish the people who did this."

After I spoke, the other people in the room, who were either friends and/or family of the father, began to talk among themselves. I have no idea what they said, but over the next few moments, the father's face began to soften. As he began to soften, his wife suddenly spoke up. Her actual words came through a translator, but I think I would have understood them even without one.

"I trust you." Followed by . . . "Please hurry."

We found the baby within three days of the abduction. The mother's mandate was simple and final, no doubt in accordance with her husband's agreement.

"We want the baby back."

On the fourth day, I returned to the parents, their baby in my arms. Never did I make a more beautiful delivery. That little baby girl returned to her designated karma, and I could return to mine.

Ultimately, the adoptive parents were given a new baby girl, and all was well. We didn't have to make any protracted explanations; they were happy to receive their little bundle of joy.

What had all of this cost me? In pure monetary terms, nearly a quarter of a million dollars. But the money doesn't matter; never did.

The beautifully spiritual end to this story is that we secured a waiver for the birth parents so they could afford to have a boy, if they so chose. The ultimate "happy ending" is that those parents became part of our organization. They have embraced the Pink Pagoda, and I embrace them.

My kingdom for a handkerchief....

24

THE GOOD, THE BAD
AND THE UGLY

Sometimes tragedy had a way of transforming itself into a gift, some-what like the birth of a phoenix from the ashes. My good friend and colleague Tim was a phoenix if there ever was one.

I first met Tim back in Canada when I was setting up another intro-ductory meeting to recruit potential teachers for my Chinese schools. My approach was to advertise in local newspapers, announcing each meeting in that particular town. Owen Sound, roughly two hours out-side of Guelph, was the site of my next presentation. Owen Sound has a population of around fifteen thousand and tended to yield some of my best recruits.

Teachers who worked for me in China could expect not only top-notch working conditions, but also optimal pay. The average Chinese teacher teaching in a Chinese school earns between 1,500 and 2,000 remenbi a month. An American or Canadian teacher in a Chinese school earns approximately 4,000 remenbi a month, roughly $900.00. A teacher in one of my schools earns 25,000 remenbi a month, and is also provided with a very comfortable apartment in one of the city's better areas. Clearly, the incentive to work in my schools was considerable.

The presentation I delivered was designed to familiarize potential candidates with what it was like to live and teach in China. If the attendees were interested, they would then sign up for an intensive, five-day TESOL course to prepare them for teaching in China. My presentations were clear, compelling, and imbued with my irrepressible, impish humor, and most people loved them. I would tell the attendees that I couldn't possibly share how much China meant to me, and that there was no way to adequately describe what they would experience if they chose to teach there. Think vague with a come-hither tone.

Most attendees just sat there and listened with enthusiasm for my words, but not always certitude for how this might work for them. Ultimately, most of them did sign up for my course, but one teacher in the back of the room seemed baited for bear. I was that bear.

He was a scrawny kind of guy dressed in one of those garish, red plaid hunting shirts, a little reminiscent of Paul Bunyan but without the stature. I took him to be about five foot six, and he had small tufts of hair arched above his ears, and very intense eyes. The others in the room seemed to know and respect him, and everyone paid close attention when he asked his first question.

"So, Dr. Garrow, I'm having trouble with your rather oblique comments about China. You love it, but we won't believe how much until we get there? Seems to me you should be giving us specifics, not just rhetoric."

"Well—and your name, sir?—if I were to tell you just how wonderful the country and people are, I'm afraid it would sound like I was exaggerating."

"You mean, like b.s.? And my name is Tim."

He fired off another couple of pointed questions, and then seemed satisfied, at least for the moment. At the end of the session, and much to my surprise, he was the first one who came up to me.

"Okay, Dr. Garrow, sign me up. I'll run down to the ATM and bring back the money. Save me a spot; please, save me a spot."

"Sure, you got it."

I had thought for sure he would be the first guy out the door; instead, he was the first to commit to the TESOL course and to teaching in China. He did take the course and passed it, and a few months later I gave him a call from China.

"Tim, Dr. Garrow here. Listen, I have a failing school here, and I've been asked by the Chinese owners to bring it up to snuff. What I need is someone to teach math, science, and English. Are you up for it?"

He didn't hesitate. I think part of his motivation was that he had grown tired of his organic strawberry business, the result of his gotten burned-out with teaching.

"You bet. When do you need me there?"

He would be leaving behind his wife, special-needs son, and two other sons who were nothing less than brilliant. Before the strawberry gambit he had been teaching in a school for the rather spoiled children of elite parents, and he was fed up with it. The failing Chinese school he would be coming to housed the children of elite Chinese parents determined to see their children gain acceptance into the most prestigious universities in North America, specifically the big three: Harvard, MIT, and the University of Toronto. The school was making overstated claims about the probability of acceptance into those schools; worse, they were "cooking the marks" so their students looked more academically accomplished than they were. Despite being offered an extravagant percentage of the school's profits because of my reputation as a marketer, I was determined to set things right.

Enter Tim. He was doing an exceptional job with his senior-year students, but clearly they were not up to the performance level being touted by the school's owners. My associate Tim and I conferred, and I concurred that he could tell the students in his class what was really going on. He told them that the Chinese owners were lying to them, and that they were in no way ready for those prestigious universities.

Immediately, we had a parents' revolt on our hands, and the parents demanded a meeting with me, the owners, and Tim. I told the truth; Tim told the truth. The owners continued to lie. My plot to make things right had to thicken. After the meeting, I called Tim aside.

"I need to fire you. I want you to come into work as usual tomorrow, and I will fire you. Then I want you to book your ticket back to Canada, and we'll see how this plays out."

The next day I resigned as principal, and now the Chinese owners were in an uproar. They offered me even more money. I said no. I also told them that I intended to call the ministry of education in Canada and advise them of what was going on. That call made it clear to me that someone was being paid off to turn a blind eye to the truth. Then the owners called Tim in Canada and offered him so much money that he agreed to return and finish the term, so the students would, in fact, be ready for their college admissions. My name was already on their certificates of achievement, and both Tim and I were determined to at least honor those students to whom we had committed at the beginning.

Tim returned out of a sense of honor and also for the big bucks the Chinese owners were willing to pay. He moved back in with me in my two-bedroom apartment for the duration, but his adventures with me were far from over. I had already watched his absolute amazement when I took him to his first Chinese Wal-mart. Unlike their counterparts in North America, those in China are multilevel, and at least two floors offer live animals and just-picked produce, from fresh bok choy to assorted fish swimming about in their own pool. Wal-mart in China is not just an American phenomenon; it's a Chinese tradition. Tim and I had also savored those wonderful teas on the general's riverboat on the Yangtze, and I would never forget his comment later that evening after we had returned home.

"You knew that tea was psychedelic, didn't you?"

I just smiled. That was the nature of our social relationship.

This next caper was an elaborate plot to return three children who had been kidnapped by their father back to their home in Canada. The man we'll call Ray was one of my teachers, but certainly not one of my favorites. He was unkempt, with shaggy blond hair but not a hint of facial hair. He was skinny, wore glasses, and his blue eyes, though intense, couldn't match the intensity of his voice, which was forceful and dogmatic. What he had done, and as people in our school were aware, was kidnap his three children from Canada and bring them with him to China, thinking that the long arm of North American law wasn't quite long enough to reach him in China. He had no concept of two words: *Garrow* and *guanxi*.

It was time for the Thanksgiving dinner that I hosted yearly for my staff. I had chosen the Marriott Hotel because I knew the chef there. He was an American, and I wanted to be able to offer my twenty-five staff members a remarkable, Western meal, complete with turkey, ham, and all the usual fixings. Tim and I arrived at the hotel, greeted by the two giant elves that were standing in the lobby. They had to have been nearly twenty feet tall. Inside the banquet room, everything was decorated to near excess with all manner of Christmas decorations, as foreshadowed by the elves in the lobby. The majority of Chinese may be Buddhists, but they love to embrace Western customs that will boost commercial profits.

Our banquet room was spectacular.

The manager seated me at the head of the long table, a position I usually eschewed. Tim sat to my left, and we had a full view of the rest of the staff members, including Ray and his three unruly children, ranging in age from five to eight. I have never seen such slovenly manners as I did in those children, but consider the source. The rest of our view included two uniformed officers, one stationed at the other end of the table, and the other standing against the wall, both in clear eyeshot of Ray, whom they were there to watch. Their presence was not without my involvement. Back at his apartment building, there was also an officer stationed on Ray's floor, just outside his door, and another at the front desk. He knew something was up, and that this banquet was serving up not only food but the real main course.

Everyone at the table except him knew what was going on, and I doubt he enjoyed one morsel of our magnificent meal. He had to be thinking, *Last Supper.*

After an evening of good food and cheer, Tim and I left together and couldn't help but smile as we watched Ray get into a cab with his children, followed right behind by more uniformed officers. He knew the game was up, and our meeting the next day would simply put the nails in his coffin.

There, in a group of uniformed officers and other law enforcement people from two continents, I made clear what his choices were: "Return to Canada with your children, or these people will handle your fate."

He knew what those consequences would be, and that one of them was especially dire. He left within days, and our team was restored to one of integrity and harmony.

Tim left to return to Canada shortly after that, with a suitcase full of cash from his short stint as the man who went from fired to phoenix. Recently, someone back in Canada asked him about me, specifically, how much could someone believe about what I said. I live large in terms of my mission to save babies, and I know there are those who doubt at least part of what they hear about my work in China, including my schools. Tim didn't miss a beat.

"Here's what I can say about Jim. Some of the small stuff may be a bit exaggerated, but the big stuff is always exactly true."

I am honored by Tim's estimation of me. May I never let him down.

25

WHO IS THIS GUY, ANYWAY?

While I never became the minister my parents wanted me to be, I have always maintained close relationships with both Christians and the Catholic Church. With the latter, I have served as a board member for *Crisis* magazine, once a major publication for Catholics around the world. Back in 1998, when the magazine was dedicating its new office building in Washington, D.C., I was invited to be a guest speaker, along with Jack Kemp. The gala was held at the Yale club, and featured a virtual who's who of top personalities, many of whom had been part of Reagan's cabinet. Being in the company of individuals ranging from Judge Bork to Cardinal Carter to Alexander Haig to Zhigniew Brzesinski to Peggy Noonan and the chief prelate from Opus Dei didn't prevent me from suggesting to Judge Bork that we put napkins over our arms and pretend to be waiters. He wasn't amused. Jack Kemp, on the other hand, was far more jovial about it.

From the time I was a small child, I was a force to be reckoned with. Physically, I was a "wee runt of a lad," born in Scotland, who then emigrated with my parents, Robert and Roberta, to Canada as a toddler. We were the first in our family to leave the country and strike out in search of opportunities on foreign soil. My mother's start in life was as the youngest of eleven children in a decidedly poor, Jewish family. In those times ,being Jewish meant ostracism in a primarily Protestant and Catholic environment. Later, when she became pregnant as a teenager, she became the ultimate social outcast in the eyes of her family and community. Such pressure might have broken most people, but not my mother. She was a battler, and her advice to me even when I was very small was to stand up for myself, for what I believed, and not be defeated by others. In particular, she had a fierce sense of justice, and always told me that it wasn't enough to speak out; you had to take action against injustice.

My father had the same kind of spirit. When his job in Canada disappeared because of government pressure from the United States, he took whatever jobs he could find, and his head never bowed. He wasn't proud; he was determined to take care of his family. The fact that a foreign government had threatened our livelihood was an omen of things to come for me in China as an adult, when I chose to defy a government mandating a one-child policy that put baby girls in deadly peril. The seeds of my adult actions were planted young by both of my parents.

There is one technical correction, here. Just last year, I found out that my father wasn't really my father. He had indeed married my mother when she was pregnant with me, but the real father was, in fact, my uncle. In reality, I started my life as an outcast. There can be tremendous power in that. Normal expectations don't apply. You can create your own destiny without the impediments of your place in society. The rebel in me started young.

When I was three, I began reading anything I could get my hands on. My mother strongly encouraged me, and by the time I was four, I was poring over the twenty-four volumes of the *American People's Encyclopedia*. I was curious about everything, and had a constant "need to know." In fact, I could be a genuine pest, as opined by so many of my teachers all the way through school.

By the time I was five, I was riding a two-wheel bike when the rest of the kids in my neighborhood were still struggling with their tricycles. No challenge was too big for me.

That attitude also inspired me to befriend and protect little Sinclair Watson, a boy from our neighborhood with whom I shared one thing in particular. We both had obvious Scottish accents, and like my mother back in Scotland, that made us different. Sinclair had an additional handicap, that one physical. He had muscular dystrophy, and the bullies in our neighborhood were always terrorizing him. Until I stepped in. I might have been small, but I was every bit as fierce as my mother in what I believed. It was wrong to hurt another person just because he was different, and I jumped in to defend my friend with both fists.

The bigger boys looked at me in disbelief. *Did this little runt of a guy really think he could fight with them?* they must have wondered. He could indeed. Maybe I couldn't manage a punch to the stomach, but I was just the right height to punch one of them on the side of his knee. Down he went, and I managed to knock them all down before they really knew—or could believe—what hit them. Defending others would become part of my mission in life, and I never pulled back because of circumstances or potential consequences. My mother had taught me that too. Just because you do the right thing and stand up for what you believe doesn't mean there won't be consequences. Those consequences are part of the equation.

In seventh grade, I took on Mr. Palmer, whose cruel treatment of those children he picked on pushed me to the edge of righteous indignation. One of those kids, Elton Horner, was the first black child in our school, and Mr. Palmer was all over him, even using his most nefarious punishment—forcing the errant gum chewer to put the offending substance in his hand and then put his hand on top of his head. At that point, Mr. Palmer would squish down the offender's hand until the gum was thoroughly embedded in the hair. A nasty mess from a nasty guy.

"Stop doing that! Stop putting people down! We don't need this!"

I stood there defiantly, unafraid of what might happen to me. What happened was predictably a trip to the principal's office and the strap. Both the principal and vice-principal Gillespie said they respected me for standing up to the teacher, but rules were rules. At home later that day, I was punished again, but both my parents respected my little act of courage.

Mr. Gillespie's words of wisdom ultimately went unheeded as I moved into adulthood: "In the future, just shut up."

Couldn't do it then; can't do it now.

As I moved into my teens, I took on another principal, whom I accused, and rightly so, of stealing money from the student council. This time my "lumps" included a visit from the RCMP (Royal Canadian Mounted Police), who were enforcing the War Measures Act that had been reinstituted by Prime Minister Trudeau. To get even with me, the principal had told them I was a drug dealer. It was a lie, but I was investigated and my room searched. It didn't matter to me; I had acted on my beliefs. I still view consequences as a fair trade for the truth. This book is about the truth, and I cannot predict the consequences. I'm ready for the lumps if those should come to pass.

Another life lesson started when I was thirteen and once again followed me into adulthood. Our family really didn't have money for anything beyond the essentials, so I got a part-time job working for Mr. Groat, who ran a variety store. On the second level of his store he ran an import business for Matchbox and Corgi toys. I was making fifty cents an hour at the beginning, but I quickly asked him to change the way I was paid. Instead of an hourly wage, he would pay me according to the orders I filled. I have a keen eye for organization and systems, and I knew that I could make his business much more profitable. He agreed; but when my salary jumped to the equivalent of seven dollars an hour, he fired me.

"Here's the lesson in life, Jim. Never look smarter than your boss."

And with that, I was terminated. Clearly, I would do better in top management or entrepreneurial endeavors. And that's exactly where I was headed.

Many years later, as a successful adult businessman, I bumped into Mr. Groat again at the Board of Trade Golf and Country Club of Toronto, located in Woodridge, where I had set up one of my Canadian schools. There, at one of those stands where a guy uses soap and water to clean the dirt and grass stains off clubs, was Mr. Groat. Years before, he had sold his business to Lesney Industries for twenty-two million dollars. Now he was a member of Weston Golf and Country Club, where the membership was a whopping one hundred thousand dollars. And here he was cleaning golf clubs and organizing golfers into foursomes.

"Mr. Groat, what are you doing here?"

He was obviously enjoying himself, and I have never forgotten his words.

"Exactly what I want to do."

My golf buddies made derisive comments about the old man, but he was smarter than any of them. When I get to be a very old man, I hope that I am able to do exactly what I want to do.

That time is very likely a long way down the road. If ever. There's always a new challenge, a new opportunity waiting around the next corner. At fourteen, that corner was in the United States, where my parents had sent me to live with my sister in Saranac, Michigan. My mother's delicate health was once again an issue, and she and I spent most of our time at loggerheads. I really didn't mind being sent away, and when I settled into school in Michigan, many lessons and opportunities were right there waiting for me.

"Jim, you're a smart kid, but you're also a smart-ass."

Mr. Gruendyke was a gruff but fair teacher, and his assessment of me was to the point.

"You have to learn to walk the line between being a smart-ass, bright kid and somebody who's got something to offer so that people will listen to you with respect."

He then gave me an opportunity to experience what those words meant. He gave me permission to show off in front of the class. It was up to me to choose how I wanted to show off. I chose the right road, and I saw firsthand what he was talking about. All those years later, when Yoda called me an ass, I could hear Mr. Gruendyke's words and I knew Yoda was right: relinquishing direct control of Pink Pagoda was the right thing to do.

From a business perspective, Saranac also led me to start two businesses both there and back in Canada—one, cleaning service station washrooms, and the other a Mr. Submarine franchise. I clearly saw that money could buy me freedom, and by the time I was just shy of my eighteenth birthday, I had amassed a true fortune of nearly $150,000.00 which had grown from both my business sales and smart stock investing with my dear friend Harry Frogley. Eventually, I would lose it all to investments gone awry and expenses from my walkabout back in the United States in the summer of 1967, but it was a great ride and an escalator to later business ventures whose profits allowed me to start Pink Pagoda and keep it alive.

Ultimately, it's not just about seeing ways to make money; it's a matter of being able to take the measure of a person. Who do you want to be involved with? Whose hands do you want to hold your fate? If I respect someone, I will go to the ends of the earth to help that person, and he or she will have my loyalty forever. Respect is my greatest motivator for saying yes to anything or anyone.

The universe knows who to challenge with obstacles and opportunities. Those events placed upon my path are an invitation to excel, to make the world better for my having been here.

God bless my mother and father. God bless Mr. Gruendyke, Mr. Gillespie, and Mr. Groat. God bless Yoda.

And God bless the children.

26

THE LORD MOVES IN MYSTERIOUS WAYS

It makes me a little nervous to say that I am a person with some special spiritual presence. My roots are most assuredly Christian, and I firmly believe that God inspires and guides my life. I also have to acknowledge that there have been too many events in my life where people—complete strangers, even—have told me that I have a powerful spiritual presence, and that I have been "chosen" to do very important work.

Perhaps it would be best to simply explain.

When I was seventeen, my curiosity led me into all kinds of adventures and inquiries. One of those was a spiritual gathering of sorts in Windsor, Ontario, just across the border from Detroit, and the audience was both Canadian and American. The overall feel of the event was yoga-inspired, and people were sitting on their mats, deep in either contemplation or formal meditation. Some were chanting; some just sat quietly. I wasn't there for the contemplative atmosphere. I was there because a friend of mine had said it would be "freaky" and full of girls. Those were the only two reasons I needed to say yes.

We arrived at the gymnasium where the gathering was being held, and were told that this was going to be a very powerful spiritual "happening," to use the cliché of the time. We sat down, just observing those around us, when a woman who seemed to be directing everything suddenly stopped talking and began to look around the room. I started looking around, too, thinking there must be something special about to occur.

"I'm afraid we can't proceed until we ask a very powerful presence to leave."

Wow, that sounded cool, and like everyone else, I started looking for whatever might be that "powerful." All I could think was that someone was definitely up the creek.

"You, the young man in green; you need to leave."

Now every head in the room was on the lookout for the guy in green, including my head. The search stopped right at my green shirt.

"You have to leave, now."

"What, me? Why do I have to leave?"

I wasn't rude or angry; I just didn't get it.

"You must leave, and take that giant angel with you."

Giant angel? All I could think about was Harvey the giant pooka, Elwood's big, rabbit-eared, imaginary friend in the film *Harvey*. I just thought it was funny, and freaky. I sat there for a minute or so, and my friend made it clear that he wasn't going to leave just because I had offended some spirit.

I stood up to go, and I swear that the room suddenly reminded me of one of those scary movies where everybody's eyes seem to glow in an otherwise dark room. The room probably held a few hundred people, but mostly I noticed their eyes from several different vantage points in the room. They didn't just seem to glow; it was more like I saw or felt hatred in their gazes.

This was not the kind of freaky I expected or wanted any part of.

I didn't so much walk as I almost stumbled my way out of the room and toward the front door. I was barely at the threshold when a man stopped me in my tracks.

"Who are you?"

"I'm Jim Garrow."

It was clear he didn't believe me.

"No, no, no. I mean, who are you *really*?"

We both stood there for what felt like at least three or four minutes, him checking me out, and me just wanting to check out of this place as fast as I could. After that, he simply went back inside the gymnasium and closed the door behind him. I stood there in disbelief, and then just walked away.

At the time, I was living back home, but I didn't say anything to anyone about what had happened. The one person with whom I could have shared the experience was my mother. Yes, she did have bouts of mental illness that today might have been diagnosed as schizophrenia, but she also had this spiritual side to her. A variety of people would come to our house, and my mum would get involved in discussions about spirituality. She spoke with a voice of authority during those discussions, and people really listened to her, even famous spiritual personalities. I was skeptical about any abilities she might have, because my experience growing up had been of a mother whose instability had caused me so much grief.

During this particular summer, my mother had visits from the Sutera twins, famous Christian evangelists from Minneapolis–St. Paul. Back in 1960, when they were teenagers just getting started with their mission, they had met my mother during one of their presentations. After that, they would show up at the house on occasion, and they and my mother would get into one of her spiritual discussions. Ravi Zacharias, an East Indian guru who was also a confrere of Billy Graham, would also drop by with his brother-in-law Sunder Krishnan to see my mother. I had grown accustomed to these people patting me on the head when I was much younger, saying things like, "God's got big plans for you, boy. Just listen to God and do what He tells you to do." I was always very polite, but their words didn't really have much impact on me then. I also had to acknowledge that purely on a spiritual plane, my mother was awesome.

One of those spiritual giants who would come by to visit was Axel Molema, a Belgian who was widely acclaimed for his architectural work at a famous company in Toronto, called Giffels. He left there in order to pursue yoga full-time, and very quickly became widely renowned for those skills.

When Axel returned this particular summer, he decided to take me on as kind of a disciple, which infuriated my mother for reasons I still don't totally understand. He had just been offered a contract to teach yoga for the Eaton family on their estate on Chamberlain Island, just north of Midland. Actually, there were four mansions on the island: Sunrise, Sunset, Eastview, and Westview. The patriarch, John David Eaton, was all crippled up from arthritis, and had to be pushed around in a wheelchair. He was a very bitter man, despite his billions of dollars in wealth. His wife, Lady Eaton, had been the one to hire Axel to come teach yoga to the rich women of Chamberlain Island, and I came along as his assistant. The contract didn't last for the full summer, because Lady Eaton became ill. Axel and I were just as glad. Those rich women were miserable to work with.

The best part of the experience was being around Axel. He reinforced what I had heard in snippets as a child, and then at that spiritual gathering where I was asked to leave, along with my "giant angel." He said that I had a significant destiny to fulfill, and that I would be guided. I can't say that I truly understood or could even accept his words to the degree he must have meant them. Only when I got to China did I see the true flowering of his pronouncement. It wasn't that I hadn't had experiences in Canada and the United States that pointed in that direction, but it was China and its people and my schools and Pink Pagoda that gave me the clarity to understand—and accept—what people had been saying to or about me all those years.

I know as deeply as I know that I'm a true Christian that I am guided and protected by a very powerful and benevolent presence. I also know that it took going to China for me to realize how profound that presence is.

The reincarnation of Dr. Norman Bethune? Chinese people, including Buddhist monks, seem to believe so. Specially chosen by God? I just follow what seems to be His Word.

What I don't have is a big, giant angel standing next to me. Or maybe I just can't see him.

26

DR. BETHUNE,
I PRESUME?

Given how revered the Bethune name is throughout China, it is ironic that in real life he was no saint.

Unlike many who choose to become doctors for reasons of altruism or dedication to a cause, Bethune wanted only to get out from under his parents' mandate that he become a minister. From an early age, he was a rebel, and his college years at the University of Toronto were far less about academics than they were about drinking, smoking, and womanizing. Back in the twenties, the University of Toronto (my alma mater) was a religious establishment that had been founded by a group of Anglicans. Most of the universities back then were religious in their foundation and mission. Today that is less prescient.

Despite all of his extracurricular activities, Bethune was nonetheless a smart guy academically and successfully went through all the rigors to become a doctor. He was also a bit of a revolutionary and a definite loudmouth. That loudmouth was on a mission to share his socialist views on Marx and Lenin. Without realizing it, he was setting up his path to China.

Before he got to China and established his ultimate destiny, he would need to make a short trip to Spain. While war raged there, he practiced as a doctor, but he also hobnobbed with generals in high society. When he extended his practice to one of the general's wives, he quickly found himself kicked out of the country. He opted for the Silk Road.

China was then engaged in a war against the Japanese, who had invaded their country. One of Bethune's friends with Chinese influence invited him to join in the resistance effort, and he found himself shipped off to the Eighth Army, which was stationed in Shijiazhuang. Shijiazhuang is the capital city of Hebei; Bethune was actually working outside the city. His mission there was to train their troops to achieve a certain level of triage and to prevent deaths from sepsis and other war-engendered injuries. He found himself teaching people how to become mini-surgeons, stemming blood flow and performing all kinds of triage. To maximize all of their efforts, he invented his own instruments, including the now standard chest spreader. All told, he developed eight different instruments for eight different patient scenarios. Accomplishments aside, he still managed to get himself in trouble because of that perennial loud mouth.

It was Bethune's accomplishments, not his behavior, that captured the attention of one Mao Tse-tung. Mao had, by then, become a paragon of Communism, and one of its tenets that Mao very much supported was internationalism. Mao believed in a one-world system, that humans are all brothers together, and that we should "commune."

When Mao heard about this doctor from Canada who was saving lives like crazy with troops in the Eighth Army, he decided to write an essay about the good doctor's accomplishments. It was only one page long, and basically said that Bethune was an example of pure Communism, of internationalism, of sacrifice for a common good, a man who should be admired and imitated.

Historically, it's unclear if the two men ever met, but the rumor persists that they did.

Meanwhile, Bethune became immortalized among those who undertook the Long March with Mao. China's new "princes apparent," Xi and Bo,* were the sons of two men who were on that Long March. Speculation was that their future regime would move back more closely to the teachings of Mao. That, of course, remained to be seen.

Against this very dramatic backdrop of war and devastation, Bethune created the prototype for the mobile army surgical hospital, better known

"The Princelings Are Coming," Economist, June 23, 2011

to the world as the *MASH*. unit. Americans in particular who still watch reruns of that iconic television series *M*A*S*H* are really looking at the handiwork of Dr. Norman Bethune. As seen in the living color of a TV screen, Bethune created the technique for transfusing blood on the battle-field. What viewers may not know is that Bethune actually used his own blood. He would literally stick a needle into his own arm and then directly transfuse it through a bottle into the Chinese soldier on the field. People were dumbfounded that such a thing could be done. It was.

People today might also be dumbfounded, flabbergasted even, to learn that Bethune died within the rigors of battle, not from an enemy's attack, but at his own hands. While operating on a patient, he cut himself, and then neglected to take care of his own wound. He died of blood poisoning. He wasn't invincible after all, but his reputation and legend live on after him, despite the fact that it was only during his last two years that his presence in the world was so remarkable. He left in that proverbial blaze of glory.

Chinese soldiers marching into battle would cry, "Attack! Baiquien is with us!"* The Chinese reference to his name is obvious; what might not be so obvious is that what they really meant was that the men would be safe going into battle, because if they were wounded, "Baiquien" would save them.

And here I am, Dr. James Garrow from Canada, who attended the University of Toronto and was a rebel all of my young life. I've always seemed to be on a mission, am radical, and have at all times stood apart from others. My driving phrase is and always has been "I'm going to do it!"

I have become to the Chinese people the new Dr. Bethune. Whether or not one wants to affirm the reincarnation aspect, which I do not, the connection between the two of us is absolutely real. Bethune saved lives on the battlefield; I save lives in towns, villages, and cities all over China.

Unlike Bethune, I am not morally profligate; and my wife, and I have been married for nearly thirty five years.

But, ah, the mouth. Or perhaps I should say, eh.

---

*"Norman Bethune: The Legend," Ville de Montréal, *http://ville.mon-treal.qc.ca/portal/page?_pageid=5437,25117626&_dad=portal&_schema=PORTAL*

It wasn't only Yoda who encouraged and exhorted me to become a mouthpiece for Pink Pagoda. It's in my blood. I will speak my mind; I will not back down if I believe I'm right. Most of the time my decisions are right, but I'm equally humble if I make a miscall.

I like to think that Dr. Bethune's spirit looks down on me with a smile, or in his case, maybe a smirk.

An exercise coach I once met back in Canada singled me out one day and offered this statement out of the blue (given that he was also a very spiritual man and a yoga practitioner, I took it as rather interesting—that word in the Chinese sense): "Jim there's something in your future that is going to be huge. Just huge. I really have a sense that you have been chosen, picked for something."

I knew that it wasn't to become a minister, although that's what everyone except me wanted me to become. Again, the Bethune connection. I just knew that the words strangely rang true. Like those from my good friend, Axel, a profound man whose wisdom I completely trusted.

"Jim, there's a real destiny for you; you're cut from a very different cloth."

That cloth is cut into a Tilley vest, and the destiny is decidedly Chinese.

28

BOUND FOR GLORY

D r. Bethune was not only bound for China; he was bound to China. So was I. The glory, if that be the right word, was never about wanting adulation or power; it was an unwritten destiny. We both accepted that destiny.

China was not on my radar when I took over at Shaw College to transform it into a profitable collegiate environment. I am an experienced educator, and I knew that I was up to the challenge. Shaw quickly became both well respected and financially stable. One of our mainstays was foreign students who wanted to acquire the best possible education in order to prepare them for commerce back in their own countries. Foremost among those at the beginning were students from Somalia, but our growing preference was to attract students from China. Their reputation as serious students was well known in educational circles, and the Chinese government was looking for a Canadian college where they could receive an optimal education.

The arrangements were made, and twenty-nine students arrived in 1995. Unlike the Somalis, so many of whom "defected" to Canada, never intending to return to their homeland, only two of the Chinese students failed to return home. The rest were diligent and high achievers. All of them came from notable families, and all were Communists. A Communist Party leader came with them, and their academics were carefully overseen, along with their behavior. They were ideal students, and I thoroughly enjoyed them.

One in particular—we'll call her Amy—was especially impressed with my educational stewardship. It wasn't long after the group returned home that I received an invitation from her to come to China. I accepted, of course, presuming the gesture was in the form of a thank-you for my good work. I was totally unprepared for what followed.

My ultimate destination was Harbin, but it would take seemingly interminable hours—nearly thirty-two of them—to reach that city. First, I would have to fly to Hong Kong, then on to Beijing, and finally to Harbin. When I arrived, there were three limousines waiting for me and enough people to fill them. Not at all what I would have expected.

I was greeted by Amy and the rest of my greeting committee, and presented with a special gift box. Such boxes are commonly used as gifts and are the harbinger of good things that can be kept in them. Mine was especially lovely, and it sits still on my desk at home.

Off we went, soon arriving at a huge banquet hall that must have seated at least a thousand people. There were banners, a profusion of food, and I was the guest of honor. I don't have words. I was also physically exhausted, but I mustered to the gala that had been prepared in my honor.

Even then, at the very beginning of my Chinese odyssey, people were treating me with a special reverence. I would understand respect; I knew that Amy had spoken most highly of me to her uncle—no one less than Hu Jintao, himself. But it was also something more. I began to sense that I was truly meant to be here, that China was my destiny, even if I had no idea how that destiny would manifest itself.

My invitation as it turned out was not only to honor me for my educational efforts back in Canada; it was also to discuss the possibility of my starting up schools in China.

In the present moment, I was being feted with foods that ran the gamut from familiar to downright wacky. I am not for the most part a big fan of Chinese cuisine, but I do enjoy dim sum. The dim sum at the banquet was excellent, especially the dim sum soup. There was also hot bok choy, and a midcourse tapioca that was positively horrid. But it was the people's faces, not the food, which are most memorable to me.

Over the next few days, I was given a tour of factories, art facilities, and all manner of commercial venues. Each day I had a special guide and a driver, and by the end of all my touring about, it was time for the Communist Party leader who had accompanied the students to Canada to ask me the big question.

"Will you help us open an English language school here in Harbin?"

What I didn't know was that there were at least eight other schools that were ready to become one of "my" schools. They were spread out all over China, including Beijing, Shanghai, Guilin, Guangzhou, and other cities. All were connected through the Communist Party. These schools were already the best; now they were about to become beyond best.

The process of setting up my operations put me in close contact with a veritable who's who of up-and-coming business and Party leaders. Even though I had not yet learned the word, I was beginning my guanxi network. I felt then as I do now that everything is ordered, and I felt guided in the work I was doing.

I knew it would be difficult to get white teachers to come all the way to Harbin, so I told the people I was working with that we had to offer high wages if we expected to get high-level teachers for our schools, whether in Harbin or elsewhere. Everyone agreed, and our schools were launched. It was time for me to return to Canada, but now there was one more thing.

"Dr. Garrow, will you stay here and run these schools for us?"

Out of the blue and into the gold, the gold being the exorbitant amount of money they were offering me if I would resign from Shaw College and stay here in China. I had already stayed three weeks beyond the original three, and I really felt that I needed to return home, at least for a while. It wasn't that my wife and my family wouldn't accept or understand any decision I made; it was about getting back to my Canadian obligations.

I did return, but a decision was already gestating that would make my decision about China easier. Despite the fact that I was continuing to honor my administrative responsibilities at Shaw College, no doubt there was a different sort of politics at play, which caused them to fire me without any real cause. I have come to believe that the deeper cause had nothing at all to do with the college.

China needed me, and there could be no obstruction. I was now free to accept my invitation to destiny.

29

BUSH NET

It was through the Christian Coalition that I came to be introduced to George Bush. The original purpose of my trip to the United States was to make a visit to Oklahoma City, where I had been invited to sit on the board of a telecommunications company. The man who had set up that connection also set up a meeting with Bush. In my confrere's words, "I think there could be a spark between the two of you."

He arranged for the four of us to have lunch: George Bush, me, a woman whose name I've forgotten, and the confrere (whose name I can't reveal). It was an upscale restaurant in Dallas, one of those "Palm" affairs, and the opening conversational banter centered around baseball. I'm not really that into baseball; definitely, more of an American thing. For Canadians, it's hockey. My only significant contribution to the sports rap was my views on the Blue Jays and the Montreal Expos. Beyond sports, we talked about the Christian Coalition, Pat Robertson, Oral Roberts, and a few other preachers. Since I personally knew Jerry Falwell, we talked about him too.

The telecommunications company was a Christian-based organization, and my confrere, himself a very well-known name in the Christian community, thought there could be a commerce connection with Bush.

At that time, my little Internet company in Canada was actually the second largest in the country. The only larger company was Sympatico, which was owned by Bell Communications. They had roughly seventy thousand customers, and I had approximately forty thousand. I was bundling my equipment with cable television companies, but the cable companies were not thinking of cooperating all the way, coast to coast. What I was doing was putting a seamless backbone across Canada, where I could outperform the United States by going through Chicago up to Guelph, Ontario. That's a short hop from the network access point (NAP) from Chicago to Guelph, and Chicago was the hub of the world's Internet. It's where all the equipment was, and the strength of the signal, its bandwidth, depletes as it hops from one network access point to another. What I was getting in Guelph was nearly instantaneous transmission. People were pinging us (checking on performance) from as far away as South America, Florida, Britain—all over the place. My Internet product was called Clean Net, because we were trying to keep children from negative influences on the Net—porn, hate literature, pedophiles, that kind of thing. That's why Bush was interested in talking about with me.

In a word, censorship.

What he and I ended up talking about was being able to take the high speed of the Internet from Chicago into Canada. Canada isn't under the control of any American law, so censorship would not be an issue. My company, International Internet Alliance, could send that high-speed signal back to the United States through the back door. In the front door, out the back door. A squeaky-clean, "scrubbed" service. I would be able to provide service to the entire United States through Canada, and all those faith-based religious groups could rest assured that their children were safe from inappropriate or dangerous material.

Bush wanted a corridor straight down from Canada to Texas, with a faster speed than was currently available in the United States. The actual structure of the organization would be to set up franchises all over Canada, but a revolt by one of those franchises resulted in my closing down the whole operation. People were looking for a way to do it themselves, and that decentralization would ruin the integrity of the whole.

Business for me is not just about money; it's about respect and loyalty. I wasn't seeing that. One miasma resolved; on to the next. This time it was the Arabs who wanted us to provide them with fiber-optic cabling, go over to the Middle East and set up their Internet system, feed it back to them from Canada, and thereby surround Israel with high-speed Internet.

My chief engineer and I went to the Marriott Hotel at the airport in Toronto, where we waited for the Arab contingency to arrive for our meeting. We all sat down, and I heard them out. I knew exactly what they were talking about, and it was all very surreptitious.

They had rented a suite, and there we sat, one of them dressed in traditional Arab clothes, the others in Western business suits.

"Well, I could probably do everything you're requesting, except for one major problem."

The Arabs looked at me quizzically.

"What might that be?"

I had two words for them.

"Gerald Bull."

Gerald Bull is the Canadian scientist who developed a cannon that could give the Arabs the ability to shoot shells from any of the Arab nations directly into Israel.

Here's what the Mossad did to Gerald Bull. He had all the work done, and he had demonstrated to the Arabs that it was workable. They were financing him. He was in Paris, France, walking up the stairs to his residence there, when the Mossad gunned him down.

The Arabs sitting across from me were not at all pleased. They were putting millions and millions of dollars on the table, and I was refusing their offer.

They didn't know Jim Garrow.

With negotiations over, I returned home. Less than a week later, the Canadian Security Intelligence Service showed up at my door, wanting to know what had happened. Satisfied that I was in no way subversive, they left, and I considered how much all of my mentors had influenced my ability to think straight and through.

Mr. Gruendyke would have been proud. So would President Bush.

30

THE NOBEL PEACE PRIZE SCANDAL

In the late fall of 2008, I received a call that would change my life in ways I could not even imagine. It was a little after eight o'clock in the evening when the call came in, and the caller I.D. gave no indication whether the call was local or long-distance. I thought it might be a telemarketer, so I certainly didn't rush to answer it. (Though I actually have a certain sympathy for those poor souls trapped at the end of a phone line, fielding abuse from angry respondents who make the telemarketer's meager earnings even more miserable.)

I picked up the receiver and was surprised, pleasantly, to discover that the voice on the other end was Chinese. The man apologized for calling so late, indicating that it was early morning in China. He explained that although he had never met me, he held me in high regard for my work in saving baby girls in China. He identified himself as the president of a well-respected university in China, and was calling to get my permission before he proceeded with something. My silence must have spurred him to cut to the chase. That silence was a seasoned response to those journalists and detractors seeking to disparage my work or trap me into saying something I shouldn't.

"Dr. Garrow, the reason I called is that I would like your permission to nominate you for the Nobel Peace Prize."

I didn't even need a feather to knock me over. The air alone was sufficient.

I mumbled something about this being such a great honor, and thanked him for his kindness. I don't even remember exactly what I said. He went on to explain that his daughter had been one of those unfortunate mothers faced with the terrible possibility of setting aside her newborn daughter. He knew that I had saved her child; and after praising God for that salvation, had sought me out.

I was still slightly suspicious that he might be looking for a way to entrap me, and had to wonder how he had been able to find the "invisible Jim Garrow." He did not share that information with me, but I thanked him anyway, and gave my permission for him to make that nomination.

"Thank you, Dr. Garrow."

And with that our conversation was over, and I went straight to my computer to find out more about this prestigious prize. While I was reasonably familiar with the parameters of the award, I was shocked to discover that only one Canadian had ever won a Nobel Peace Prize. Just one? I was more than just a little incredulous. What I also didn't know was that the names of those who are nominated but don't win are not revealed for fifty years. I didn't then, nor do I now, understand the logic behind that proscription.

I immediately told my wife, and she was as shocked as I was. The next day I shared my nomination with my former minister, and he concurred with my caller that I was indeed worthy of such a nomination, and that my devoted work to saving baby girls from gendercide was just the kind of accomplishment that deserved recognition from the Nobel Committee.

After that, I went about my daily routines with the thought of my nomination hovering somewhere between an interesting possibility and a nod from God. Ultimately, the announcement came in 2009 that President Barack Obama had been awarded the prize, and my mood went from quiet appreciation to a certain kind of indignation. Not because I personally did not win, but because this man in particular had been given the ultimate "peacemaker's" prize. Further, I found it cruelly ironic that the monies gifted by Nobel were drawn from his patents for both dynamite and explosive devices. Expiation, perhaps? It was a double hit that may have gone somewhat unnoticed by me had it not been for my own nomination.

I do realize how that must sound. I don't need an award to know and feel that the work I do with Pink Pagoda is the consummate work of a peacemaker. I don't need to have the world ooh and aah over me when what sustains me is the thought of one more smile that won't be extinguished by a cruel law. It's certainly not about the money; my Chinese schools and ancillary investments provide for both me and Pink Pagoda.

It's about injustice at any level, especially when it costs the lives of innocent people. For the most part, I agree with the past choices made by the Nobel Committee. In my opinion, 2009 represents a radical departure from those choices. By no means—and I say this not as a Canadian but as a citizen of the world—is Barack Obama a peacemaker. Enough said.

To my own mission in life, I thank God for the possibilities of each new day. Has Pink Pagoda saved a future Mother Teresa, Frida Kahlo, Margaret Thatcher, Clara Schumann, or Marie Curie? We can never know for sure the impact of forty thousand baby girls' lives who have created a new hope, not just for China but for the world. And there are more baby girls to come.

I will continue as God's instrument. I will do whatever He asks, whatever is required. I do not need a man's prize to continue with my mission. As Mother Teresa told me, "Our hands are the hands of God ministering his love to those in need. For some, we are the only Jesus they will ever encounter."

I fold my hands in prayer and gratitude.

PRESIDENT BARACK OBAMA

THE WHITE HOUSE

WASHINGTON, D.C.

NOVEMBER 3, 2009

Mr. President:

I would like to congratulate you on your 2009 Nobel Peace Prize victory. As with all victories there are those who were in the race and did not win the gold medal. The Bethune Institute and its Pink Pagoda program, saving baby girls from infanticide in the People's Republic of China, got the silver medal. The win or loss is not what is important here, but whether the world will see the end to one of the most devastating of policies that have resulted in the deaths of 23,000,000 females (the demographics show this). China's one-child policy should end now and I believe that you can help to bring about its end as surely as Ronald Reagan brought about the end of the Soviet Union. The "tear down this wall" line in his speech at the Brandenburg gate is long remembered as President Reagan's finest moment. I would posit to you a scenario in which President Obama seizes the world stage in his acceptance speech for the Nobel Peace Prize. "President Hu, stop the war against China's daughters and end the one-child policy today," could be a magnificent answer to the many questions of the prematurity of this award. You would be using this stage as a call for the end of a barbaric practice that is promulgated by a forced government policy. This policy has skewed the demographics for the nation and produced a real quandary for Chinese leadership. I believe that they would love to end this policy and would partner with you to see its end. All you have to do is ask.

When I was in Grade 8 attending Kentwood High School in Grand Rapids, Michigan, I had a history teacher named Mr. Groendyck who challenged us to go beyond ourselves and make a mark on history itself. He said that "one man, can change the world." Years later, my mother became ill and I was sent to school in Saskatchewan, Canada, where I was challenged by the sacrifice of Dr. Norman Bethune, an internationalist who had come to the aid of the Chinese 8th Army effort against the Japanese invasion of China. He died as a result of blood poisoning and was memorialized by Chairman Mao where Bethune was praised as an example of the "true internationalist spirit and true Communist." All Chinese school children memorize this essay in the equivalent of Grade 9. Later in life, I founded the Bethune Institute and for the past 10 years have been saving baby girls from the aftermath of the misguided "one child policy" in China. We have saved 31,161 girls to date at a personal cost of $23 million dollars.

We may have lost the Nobel Peace Prize to you, President Obama, but I believe that there is a higher purpose to every event in our lives. The universe is indeed unfolding as it should. I have been audacious in my challenge to you and the hope I have is that you will respond and use the opportunity to show the stature of a great world leader unafraid to speak truth to power and change the world for the better.

Our prayers go with you.

Sincerely,

DR. JIM GARROW

EXECUTIVE DIRECTOR

THE BETHUNE INSTITUTE AND PINK PAGODA

31

DR. JAMES GARROW DOESN'T EXIST

The rumors of my life have been exaggerated. At least that's what at least two noted American journalists in China have asserted in trying to find out more about the man behind Pink Pagoda.

"He doesn't exist."

I am here to say that I certainly do exist. The residents of Guelph, Ontario, will be the first to tell you that they know who I am, and that I am recognized throughout the town. Were I back in Chongqing, I would be widely recognized there as well. There are also a number of people in New York and other parts of the United States among whom mine would be a familiar face.

Alas, my work with Pink Pagoda has caused me to lose access to both China and the United States. After the announcement of my nomination for the Nobel Peace Prize in 2009, both borders were closed to me. I can only speculate as to who might be behind such proscription, but it doesn't really matter. The result would still be the same. What's most important is that Pink Pagoda is flourishing, and my spirit travels with every baby who is placed on both continents.

There is also the issue of this book. Once it was known that my book had been sold, it wasn't long before I received a phone call from someone in China. Two words.

"Be careful."

I held on to the publisher's contract for nearly a week, discussing the situation with both my family and friends and my literary agent. We all agreed. The book had to be published.

The Chinese know that I would never say anything to dishonor anyone in their country. I'm also a foreigner. I'm still a foreigner. That's very important to understand. I've never become Chinese in the legal sense. I've never taken on Chinese citizenship. One might think that citizenship would be an important, well-advised step; that someone who loves China as much as I do would want to become one of its citizens. I know better. There is power in being who and what I am. There is huge safety in my Canadian citizenship. Especially given what is happening in China right now.

At present, Hu Jintao is still in power. By all indications the new president will be Xi, and the new prime minister, Bo. Xi in particular is a direct throwback to the ideologies of Mao Tse-tung. Xi may be Harvard and Oxford, and dress in Western clothes, but in this case, clothes most certainly do not make the man. As I've said before, his father was on the Long March, as was Bo's. Their sensibilities are firmly Communist. In schools across China, Xi is bringing back Communist Party songs, reinvigorating the patriotic Communist. He's very young, and the old guard is just standing back, observing. Hu Jintao was the youngest leader ever to hold the highest position in China. Xi is right there behind him, ready to return China to its Communist roots.

As part of that return, only Chinese heroes are now being celebrated. That is Xi's directive. I may be a hero to the Chinese people who know of me, but I am most definitely not a hero in Xi's eyes. Even Mao's one-page treatise about Dr. Bethune is no longer taught in schools. Again, Xi's doing. There is no welcome for a Canadian hero on Chinese soil, even if the work I do is known to be saving human lives. I am forever a foreigner.

So, I'm here in Guelph, still supplying monies to Pink Pagoda, occasionally talking to Yoda's son on the phone. He is eminently pleased that his father will be honored in this book. It saddens him that I cannot come back and visit, but we both know what would happen if I were allowed back in the country. I would be arrested as a criminal who engages in illegal activities. On Canadian soil, I can be a "criminal" with impunity.

I was arrested once, detained actually, when trying to cross the border into Hong Kong. That was midway into Pink Pagoda, and if it hadn't been for Hu Jintao's sister, I would have been formally arrested and detained. I hadn't realized that my passport was expired, and I found myself being roughly handled while I tried to figure out how I would be able to quickly come up with what amounts to nearly thirty thousand dollars, in cash, for my fine. To the rescue came that dear woman, and I was once again a free man. But it was an omen. *"Be careful, Jim."*

I was and I am. Pink Pagoda needs me.

32

LEGACY

In the introduction of this book, I spoke of the many circumstances that would change in China and other countries as a result of the fact that more than forty thousand little girls would live whose lives came very close to being expendable as a direct result of the one-child policy in the People's Republic. Over the course of the past fifteen years, my direct involvement in China and with its people has provided me with an understanding of the personal pain of the tragedy and its horrific numbers. The estimates range from 5 to 8 million young girls murdered annually, and those estimates do not include sex selected abortions. The *Economist* published the incredible numbers that the now-skewed population figures show us. Where a 104 to 100 ratio (males to females) would be normal, Chinese numbers are now more on the order of 126 to 100. This is an incredible imbalance and quite unnatural. The societal consequences are dramatic and long-term.

With the death of our incredibly wise and connected Yoda, we suffered a loss of immense impact to each and every member of the Pink Pagoda community. But our overall legacy was challenged and changed by this gentleman in ways that guaranteed our continued existence and success in saving many more girls than we ever could have dreamed. As a planner and architect of the structures and procedures that we developed and used, Yoda was a Michelangelo. This artist understood how things should look, how to draw the eye of the observer, and ultimately what the finished product should be. He wisely chose the people who were best for the tasks at hand and trained them well. His simple loyalty to the task and his preparation of the next generation in leadership and the loyal troops who serve this small army was brilliantly done.

The Pink Pagoda organization is not large, but it is a totally different entity when compared to what we were at the beginning. Well-intentioned but haphazard, dependent on luck for the most part, and seriously close to self-destruction. We did what we could with what we had. We had many couples desperate to save their children and many desperate couples wanting a baby to raise as their own. When Yoda took the reins, he immediately began to reorganize the structure and methods and built safeguards that utilized his intelligence background as the well from which the organization drew its sustenance. I provided the funds to carry the work on the financial end, and we very carefully expanded our reach into many levels of government and the military. At every turn we had caring, loving people who stepped up to help as the need arose. We were careful to steer clear of the religiously based community, as they were a target of so many levels of government that they would have imploded the organization very quickly. And the organization today is nothing like the organization in its beginning stages. We are a lean, mean, cell-based machine. Our ability to successfully intervene for the children has seen us develop a network capable of taking care of as many as are brought to us. With a waiting list of more than eighty-five thousand interested and available families waiting for their own child, we could not begin to fill the demand.

Let us reiterate a basic concept here. We are not a charity, but rather a philanthropic work, funded totally by me. We do not accept funds from anyone. The adoptive parents pay us nothing. We take care of all expenses for the exchanges and have our education fund set up for each child. A deposit of $100 USD is made to our education account for each child. That is invested along with all the other funds, and the interest or "profits" from a variety of financial vehicles has helped the fund grow exponentially. This money has been able to provide for medical expenses for those families who needed corrective surgery on their adoptive girls and could not afford the procedure. We covered those expenses, again not expecting or asking for any repayment. There have been rare occasions where other expenses that came to our attention were also met through the fund. Keep in mind that the fund has had one hundred dollars times forty thousand ($100 x 40,000) deposited to it over the course of the eleven years since its inception. That in itself is four million dollars, and it has not sat in a bank account. The invested funds grew substantially, especially when one investment in the Chinese telecommunications industry netted a 3,000 percent increase in a two-year period. I wish we had more of the fund invested in it, but it was a substantial holding on our part. The education fund is now larger than the overall costs for the entire Pink Pagoda program since day one. How did this happen? I run the risk of having some of you who do not believe in the hand of God intervening in the affairs of men, and girls, turning us off at this point. But believe me, my personal finances could not hold a candle to this growth. Clear and almost clairvoyant moves were made by our money managers that leave you scratching your head and thanking a gracious God for His generosity and guidance. Our girls are provided for. I am a great believer in the biblical reproof, "Ye have not, because ye ask not" (James 4:2). The things I have asked for in prayer are nothing short of the miraculous. The answers have been consistently yes.

Do we project numbers into the future of the girls that we will save? No. We have a mandate and a mission that says that we will accept every girl we are given with the caveats that Yoda has put in place that protect our integrity and our individuals and mission. We have a responsibility now for more than ten among our ranks who because of age or infirmity have not been able to continue on and are retired. We continue to pay the salaries of our folks who were murdered and will until their families no longer have need. We continue to disperse huge sums in guanxi payments to government, police, and other officials who aid us in our work. We carry the expenses and salaries of our workers as well as provide contingency funds for the unexpected eventualities, because even in work that we believe is ordained of God, Murphy's Law holds sway. If something can go wrong, it will, and we try to have a plan for it.

Yoda was a godsend and a very intelligent leader. His son has proven time and time again to be even brighter than his father and just as well placed. His organization is built on the foundation of his father's successful career and contacts, which he has inherited and expanded. We are in good hands. Since the loss of our faithful workers, the loyalties of our folks have deepened, and each is willing to give his or her life to the cause. I have the privilege of counting 148 brave souls as friends and comrades in this great endeavor.

God bless them and keep them.

Aas a result of wise counsel and with the portent of this book hitting the shelves and the sudden interest of movie folks, we have been challenged to create a 501-C-3 organization that would allow the rest of the world to join us in the efforts. The name, of course, is Pink Pagoda LLC. You can learn more about how you can help our brave Chinese compatriots in their mission to save baby girls from gendercide at our internet site, www.pinkpagoda.org.